THE PEOPLE'S VERDICT

About Policy Network

Policy Network is an international thinktank and research institute. Its network spans national borders across Europe and the wider world with the aim of promoting the best progressive thinking on the major social and economic challenges of the 21st century.

Our work is driven by a network of politicians, policymakers, business leaders, public service professionals, and academic researchers who work on long-term issues relating to public policy, political economy, social attitudes, governance and international affairs. This is complemented by the expertise and research excellence of Policy Network's international team.

A platform for research and ideas

- Promoting expert ideas and political analysis on the key economic, social and political challenges of our age.
- Disseminating research excellence and relevant knowledge to a wider public audience through interactive policy networks, including interdisciplinary and scholarly collaboration.
- Engaging and informing the public debate about the future of European and global progressive politics.

A network of leaders, policymakers and thinkers

- Building international policy communities comprising individuals and affiliate institutions.
- Providing meeting platforms where the politically active, and potential leaders of the future, can engage with each other across national borders and with the best thinkers who are sympathetic to their broad aims.
- Engaging in external collaboration with partners including higher education institutions, the private sector, thinktanks, charities, community organisations, and trade unions.
- Delivering an innovative events programme combining in-house seminars with large-scale public conferences designed to influence and contribute to key public debates.

www.policy-network.net

THE PEOPLE'S VERDICT

Adding Informed Citizen Voices to Public Decision-Making

Claudia Chwalisz

policy network

ROWMAN &
LITTLEFIELD
INTERNATIONAL

London • New York

Published by Rowman & Littlefield International Ltd
Unit A, Whitacre, 26-34 Stannary Street, London, SE11 4AB
www.rowmaninternational.com

Rowman & Littlefield International Ltd. is an affiliate of Rowman & Littlefield
4501 Forbes Boulevard, Suite 200, Lanham, Maryland 20706, USA
With additional offices in Boulder, New York, Toronto (Canada), and Plymouth (UK)
www.rowman.com

British Library Cataloguing in Publication Data

A catalogue record for this book is available from the British Library

ISBN: PB 978-1-78660-436-1
ISBN: eBook 978-1-78660-437-8

Library of Congress Cataloging-in-Publication Data
Library of Congress Control Number: 2017941124

∞™ The paper used in this publication meets the minimum requirements of
American National Standard for Information Sciences—Permanence of Paper for
Printed Library Materials, ANSI/NISO Z39.48-1992.

Printed in the United States of America

CONTENTS

ACKNOWLEDGEMENTS

This publication is the output of an extensive research study generously supported by Professor Tony Crook, who funds the Crook Public Service Fellowship, a programme for the Faculty of Social Sciences at the University of Sheffield, which was based at the Sir Bernard Crick Centre in its first year. Thanks also go to the ESRC and Policy Network, particularly Patrick Diamond, for supporting this work. Robert Philpot and Ben Dilks have been astute and patient editors. I would also like to thank Dhara Snowden and the team at our publishers, Rowman & Littlefield International.

An important note of thanks also goes to the individuals whom I interviewed, for their time, advice and stimulating reflections. Peter MacLeod, the principal of MASS LBP, as well as Luca Belgiorno-Nettis and Iain Walker, the founder and director of the newDemocracy Foundation, deserve a particular mention for their generosity in time and in putting me in contact with the individuals from various public authorities who were interviewed for the case studies. Peter's team at MASS LBP, where I was kindly invited to spend some time on my research trip to Canada, were also immensely helpful. Thanks to Chris Ellis, Alex Way and Danielle Johnston especially.

Not everybody that I interviewed for this research wished to be referenced. However, thank you to Fiona Cavanagh, Daniel Fusca,

viii ACKNOWLEDGEMENTS

Judy Pfeifer, Giles Gherson, Phil Simeon, Tony Dean, Sam Erry, Brian Fior, Tannis Fenton, Andreas Laupacis, Jonathan Rose, Michael Pal, Matt Ryan, Dan Popping, Gail Fairlamb, and Jo Davie for valuable exchanges about your involvement in various long-form deliberative processes.

A notable mention also goes to those who helped shape my theoretical thinking behind this work and for providing reflections on the UK aspects of this work. Oliver Escobar, Matthew Taylor, Geoff Mulgan, Eddie Molloy, Graham Smith, Paul Kirby, Matt Wood, and David Farrell all offered valued feedback.

FOREWORD

Matthew Flinders

The recent decision by lexicographers at Oxford Dictionaries that 'post-truth' is their international word of the year is a sad reflection on the state of democratic politics. The word is defined as "relating to or denoting circumstances in which objective facts are less influential in shaping opinion than appeals to emotion and personal belief". Apparently the use of the phrase has surged by 2,000% in the last 12 months and gained further momentum during the Brexit referendum in the United Kingdom and the presidential election in the United States. At a time of growing public distrust with facts and information offered by experts (including academics) it may well be that 'post-truth' becomes one of the defining phrases of the next decade. If it does, it will join an established narrative concerning 'post-democracy' and the sense that democratic politics has to a large extent mutated into a closed, elitist world in which elected politicians have few powers in an increasingly interdependent and economically aggressive world. A public attachment to what it feels is 'post-truth' politics is therefore little more than a symptom of the deeper political malady known as 'post-democracy'.

The question then becomes one of how to close the gap that seems to have emerged between the governors and the governed and in this regard The People's Verdict offers a fresh set of ideas and new options for revitalising democratic politics. By focusing on long-form deliberative processes, it tackles the issue of scale in a very direct manner. Visions of returning to some modern version of Athenian democracy at the local level in which the majority of citizens take part in debates and decisions tend to be naïve in theory and fail to acknowledge just how severe the current situation is in terms of disengagement. At the other end of the democratic scale, the use of referendums is equally problematic. As the European Union referendum in the UK revealed, they tend to polarise opinion into crude and false choices between 'left' or 'right', 'leave' or 'stay', 'black' or 'white'. They offer little room for the simple fact that democratic politics revolves around shades of grey and the production of compromises that inevitably represent something of a fudge. And yet this is not the failure of politics. Its ability to produce compromise – even though its processes might be slow and cumbersome, the grate and grind, they will never satisfy everyone all of the time – is the beauty of politics, not its failure.

Concern about the crisis of democracy is not a new phenomenon. The Trilateral Commission's major report, The Crisis of Democracy, was published in 1974. Bernard Crick's seminal In Defence of Politics appeared over a decade before that and remains arguably more important today than when it was published over 50 years ago. What has been missing, however, from the vast literature on the 'end', 'suicide' or 'crisis' of democracy is any practical analysis of the middle-ground somewhere between local micro-politics, at one end, and blunt referendums, at the other. This is exactly why The People's Verdict is such an important publication at a particularly opportune moment in political history. It offers a fresh democratic tool through which to engage with the public, but in a meaningful and sophisticated manner. Indeed, public engagement on its own is of little value to democracy: informed public engagement, however, is the lifeblood of democracy.

Phrased in this manner the use of long-form deliberative practices provides a way to devolve power to randomly selected groups of citizens and, through this, develop a deep awareness of the challenges and opportunities presented by the issue under discussion. But there is a deeper, more fundamental role that such initiatives can play in terms of creating new democratic spaces that actually inspire and build new communities and active citizens. I know this from my own experience helping to deliver the Democracy Matters project in 2015–16. The initiative, discussed in this publication, created two fairly large long-form deliberative processes to explore the government's plans for regional government in England. A fairly typical framework was adopted based around discrete phases of activity, but one of the most surprising elements of the project was the manner in which it sparked democratic energy and engagement that lived on well beyond the formal timescales of the project. This flows into a wider point about the rise of so-called 'anti-political' sentiment. I travel the world working on specific projects and meeting a broad range of social groups and I am yet to meet anyone or any group that is genuinely 'anti-political'. Everyone I meet believes in the need for some form of political system, but they have often grown frustrated or despondent with the existing model. They are, therefore, not 'anti-political' but actually 'pro-a-different-form-of-politics'. They want to 'do' politics differently and long-form deliberative processes provide a way of 'doing' politics differently.

No one is arguing that these mechanisms provide a panacea for the challenges of democratic governance. Just like democratic politics itself, long-form deliberative processes "cannot make all sad hearts glad" (to paraphrase Crick) but they can play a positive role in terms of deepening and revitalising politics. They also provide new channels and opportunities for civic involvement, place some responsibility back in the hands of citizens, and their findings are likely to be taken seriously by politicians and respected by the wider public. Long-form deliberative processes will not deliver easy or pain-free solutions to complex social or political challenges for the simple reason that easy or pain-free solutions do not exist. And yet injecting the people's verdict through the use of carefully planned and adequately resourced deliberative mechanisms will undoubtedly strengthen the decision-making process in terms of legitimacy and may produce fresh and innovative ideas. It may also play an important role in shifting the nature of politics away from the thin, cosmetic 'post-truth' emphasis that appears to have arisen and back towards a deeper more 'evidence-based' or 'truth-based' form of democratic dialogue.

Matthew Flinders, director of the Sir Bernard Crick Centre for the Public Understanding of Politics and professor of politics at the University of Sheffield.

EXECUTIVE SUMMARY

This book argues that long-form deliberations help public bodies to legitimise difficult decisions and make effective policy. Based on comparative research into 48 case studies from Canada and Australia, it draws lessons for the United Kingdom given the similar culture and Westminster-style of government political institutions shared between the three countries.

The key finding is that by putting the problem to the people and giving them information and time to discuss the options, find common ground and decide what they want, public bodies gain the legitimacy to act on hard choices.

The sheer number of examples from Canada and Australia also disprove many of the common arguments against involving citizens in important public decisions. They demonstrate that people are indeed capable of deliberating on complex issues and of offering realistic and pragmatic solutions. As Peter MacLeod, Luca Belgiorno-Nettis, Iain Walker and countless others involved in organising and running long-form deliberative processes will attest, the public is a resource to be tapped, not a risk to be managed.

Canadian and Australian premiers, ministers, mayors and other public authorities have been using this approach to make important decisions for close to a decade. They range from developing

Melbourne's 10-year, $5bn budget to designing a 30-year infra-
structure investment strategy in the State of Victoria and updating
Ontario's condominium legislation based on the input of owners and
dwellers.

In also examining the key forms of public consultation often used
in the UK, this book highlights that long-form deliberative processes
often cost a modest amount of money and last less time than commissions, inquiries and referendums. In other words, there is a more
efficient way of solving problems in a democracy.

Finally, long-form deliberative processes need not be limited to
local issues. Once again, the wide array of examples indicates that
involving citizens in public decision-making can lead to influential
change at the city, regional and national levels too.

Moreover, with regional devolution on the agenda in the UK, this
is an opportune moment to consider how long-form deliberations
can be an important feature of the new institutions being created.
Canadian and Australian policymakers, politicians and civil servants
have been leading the way in leveraging the wisdom of ordinary
citizens to make well-crafted policies that the public supports. When
citizens collaborate, learn, debate with experts and empathise with
one another, sound public judgement is more likely to prevail. While
efforts to use new forms of citizen engagement do exist in the UK,
notably by innovative local councils and devolved parliaments, the
benefits of the rigorous long-form deliberative approach are yet to
be reaped, let alone institutionalised. The opportunity to do so is
immense.

INTRODUCTION

After three years of consultation, debate and research, and at a cost of £20m, the Airports Commission released its long-awaited report on expansion in 2015: Heathrow or Gatwick. It concluded that expanding Heathrow was the best option after all. At last – the eternal debate was over! Masked by the cloak of an independent commission, the government could finally act. It no longer mattered that the former prime minister, David Cameron, had pledged in 2009: "The third runway at Heathrow is not going ahead, no ifs, no buts". The government accepted the commission's proposals. Expansion is currently under way.

Not quite. The time-consuming and costly commission was merely one delaying tactic for making a complex and controversial decision. Bedevilled by politics, the time to decide was pushed back once again until after the London mayoral elections in May 2016. Heathrow is, after all, surrounded by Tory marginal seats. In fact, it was not until September 2016 that the new prime minister, Theresa May, finally approved the runway expansion, only for a new public consultation on the impact of the third runway to be announced. Members of Parliament will have an opportunity to vote in the winter of 2017–18.

This is not a problem specific to the Conservative party, however. For about half a century, British politicians of all political leanings have dithered on the issue. The debate seems endless. In fact, this was the sixth commission or inquiry looking into the pros, cons and costs of airport expansion since the Wilson government set up the Roskill Commission in 1968. With almost every new government, plans were scrapped, a new consultation was initiated and new recommendations were given. A dog chasing its tail. Ultimately, Cameron delayed indefinitely until he stood down as leader, leaving the choice to his successor. Like her predecessors, May has also chosen to defer responsibility to another consultation.

This frustrating scenario begs the question: how should we solve complex and difficult problems in a democratic society?

The default and unquestioning response in our system of representative democracy is that we leave these decisions to elected politicians; our representatives. Their role is to study and decide the issues that most ordinary citizens have neither the time nor the knowledge to consider themselves. At first it may seem that declining levels of trust in politicians has stripped them of legitimacy, leaving them paralysed and with no choice but to delegate their responsibility to independent bodies. Yet the arc of history shows that this practice is nothing new. It is inherent to the system. Between 1945 and 2000, there were 37 royal commissions in the United Kingdom – 34 of which took place before 1979. More recently, the model of the royal commission has been truncated into more rapidly reporting inquiries. At least in theory; inquiries are meant to last no more than 18 months. In reality, they have often lasted longer than commissions. For instance, the Iraq inquiry announced its findings almost seven years after it started investigating. Since 2000, there have been four commissions and 48 inquiries (The National Archives).

Electoral incentives sometimes trump the desire to act for the public good. As the president of the European commission, Jean-Claude Juncker, famously said: "We all know what to do, we just don't know how to get re-elected after we've done it". Creating commissions on the same topic every few years is thus not purely a means of seeking impartial advice, it is also a political delaying tactic. This is particularly so if the commission is intended to report after an election. It is also costly and, as demonstrated by the airport expansion example, often ineffective at building public support and democratic legitimacy for the decision. Is there not a better way?

The latest vogue in handing over responsibility for tough decisions is equally illusory: referendums. Befitting the populist mood of letting 'the people' decide, it also reflects a distrust of political representatives. But referendums are not an accurate way of finding out what 'the people' want. Complex issues are boiled down to a binary, 'simple' choice. Most individuals do not have the time or the resources to become familiar with all of the nuanced arguments. Ahead of the UK's referendum on the European Union, only 16% of voters said they felt 'very well informed' or 'well informed' ahead of the vote (Electoral Reform Society, 2016). Few voters properly understand how the European commission works, the role of the European council, or the impact of EU policies on their daily lives. Moreover, the victors are then left to interpret the 'true meaning' of the result which, as witnessed after the Brexit referendum, meant different things to different people. May herself has even claimed that "when the British people voted in the referendum last June, they did not simply vote to withdraw from the European Union; they voted to change how the country works . . . forever" (*Daily Telegraph*, 8 January 2017). Many would contest this interpretation.

Furthermore, often people vote in referendums for reasons that have little to do with the question being asked. In the EU referendum, some may have voted because they did not like Cameron, the government's policies on other issues, notably immigration, or as a vote against the metropolitan 'elite', seen to be largely in favour of staying in. As the public votes for myriad reasons, it is impossible to win a mandate for a detailed answer to a simple question. Moreover, a vote in favour of the status quo does not necessarily mean the issue is 'closed'. After the independence referendum in Scotland, nationalists are calling for another poll, while millions signed a petition for a second EU referendum that would require a supermajority and a minimum turnout.

Arguably, none of these methods – independent commissions, inquiries and referendums – is an efficient or particularly democratic way of resolving crunchy dilemmas. There is an alternative route, however, of elected representatives involving ordinary people in more ambitious engagement processes. Directly involving a randomly selected, representative group of citizens in the decision-making process can help resolve the dual efficiency and legitimacy crisis faced by traditional approaches.

LONG-FORM DELIBERATIONS

For some, the terms 'deliberative mini-publics,' 'democratic innovations,' 'collaborative governance' and 'participatory governance' – among others – will come to mind (Grönlund et al. 2014; Ryan and Smith 2014; Smith 2009; Fung and Wright 2001; Fung 2006, 2015; Goodin and Dryzek 2006; Fishkin 2009; Ansell and Gash 2008). These expressions loosely refer to the use of mechanisms that directly engage citizens (as opposed to representatives or organised interests) in the public decision-making process. They differ when it comes to the emphasis on deliberation or representativeness; on the scale (size of group, length of deliberations); the method of participant selection (random or self-selection); and the intended purpose (educative, advisory, or decision-making). They vary from participatory budgeting, to deliberative polls, consensus conferences, citizens' juries, citizens' assemblies and 21st century town hall meetings. All of them can be described under the umbrella term of 'democratic innovations' (Elstub and Escobar, forthcoming 2018).

In many ways, the idea of greater citizen engagement in public decision-making is nothing new. Anyone even remotely familiar with this territory has probably read numerous times about the 1980s Porto Alegre example of participatory budgeting. But none of these quite encapsulate a method used to efficiently solve complex and difficult policy problems. Participatory budgeting is often limited to the local level, is hampered by self-selection (limiting representativeness and diversity of perspectives) and does not follow one strict methodology. Deliberative polls have most often been academic exercises rather than decision-making tools deployed by people in authority. Citizens' juries usually involve only 12 to 24 people who meet over a very short period of time, typically one to two days. Consensus conferences are typically limited to focusing on controversial scientific and technological developments and, like citizens' juries, only involve around 15 people who meet for a few days in a row. Citizens' assemblies involve many more people (around 100 or more), last a much longer period of time (around a year) and have often been used for constitutional questions. They are also expensive. And 21st century town hall meetings are a targeted mobilisation of up to 5,000 citizens who meet for one day. They fall prey to the same self-selection problem as participatory budgeting and are not focused or long enough for solving complex issues.

There is, however, another method, a new type in the growing and evolving family of mini-publics: long-form deliberative processes (a phrase originally coined by Peter MacLeod of MASS LBP in Canada). They are a middle way between the citizens' jury and the citizens' assembly – a larger group of randomly selected people than the jury (24 to 48), meeting for a shorter amount of time than the assembly, but for a longer period of time than the jury (two to three months). The use of this method has proliferated in the past few years, particularly in two countries fairly similar to the UK in terms of political culture and institutions: Canada and Australia.

Since 2010, there have been almost 50 examples in the two countries – at all levels of governance and on a variety of serious, difficult and important questions. In Canada, long-form deliberative processes tend to be called citizens' reference panels, citizens' assemblies or citizens' commissions. In Australia, the preferred term is citizens' jury. But the confusing difference in vocabulary masks a similarity in semantics. In both countries, the process is remarkably comparable, with a key set of characteristics distinguishing these methods from other forms of consultation or citizen engagement under the 'democratic innovations' umbrella. For the purposes of clarity, the overarching term to describe these will be 'long-form deliberations'. They are characterised by the following criteria:

* Citizens are asked by someone with authority (usually a minister, a mayor, a council, a government agency, etc.) to help solve a pressing problem. It should involve trade-offs and more than one solution should be possible and realistic. Crucially, there is no predetermined objective.
* The group is composed of a small number (usually 24 to 48) of randomly selected citizens from the community (this can be the national, regional or local community depending on the scope of the question).
* The group of citizens commits to spending a longer period of time – usually meeting four to six times over the course of two to three months – learning about and deliberating on a policy issue from many different angles.
* They are not asked to give their own opinion on the issue (a crucial difference to focus groups and most consultations), but to deliberate on behalf of their community. Their aim is to reach a consensus.
* They propose a set of concrete recommendations to the policymakers and politicians, who respond directly and publicly to each proposal.

THE AIM OF THIS BOOK

This book seeks to explore whether the use of long-form deliberations could be a more efficient and democratic way of resolving tricky policy dilemmas than the route of commissions, inquiries or referendums or more traditional public consultation forms such as town hall meetings. Would it cost less money? Would it give the government the capacity to overcome political paralysis and act? Would it result in greater legitimacy for controversial decisions taken by politicians?

It will also consider the following questions: Are there certain types of policies which are better suited to be developed in this way? Can long-form deliberations be an effective policymaking model at various levels of governance? What are the conditions for success?

The focus is on a case study analysis of long-form deliberations in Canada and Australia since 2010, of which there are almost 50 cases to consider. It is also arguable that both countries have a similar political culture to the UK, so the conclusions drawn can be comparable. The findings will be linked to how the same policy dilemmas have been resolved in the UK – was there a royal commission or an inquiry instead? How efficient was the process? Did it give the government the legitimacy to act? Or is it like the airport expansion scenario, where it has taken almost 50 years since the first commission on the topic for progress to be made?

The first section considers the theoretical framework in which these questions are considered and outlines the methodology used. The second section is in two parts – learning from best practice in Canada and in Australia. There is an overview of the costs, duration, topics covered and outcomes of all of the long-form deliberations, followed by five in-depth case studies from each country. The third section considers lessons from the UK. First, how efficient and effective commissions, inquiries and traditional public consultation have been at solving crunchy policy dilemmas. Second, it reflects on New Labour's experiments with citizens' juries and why they did not catch on, what has changed since then, and other (mostly academic) trials of various deliberative mini-publics. Finally, the last section offers a conclusion and recommendations, outlining the optimum conditions, types of policy questions best suited, and the incentives for government to choose this method over other, well-worn paths.

THEORETICAL FRAMEWORK AND METHODOLOGY

The three strands of theory that have influenced the thinking in this book are predominantly cultural or social coordination theory (Douglas, 1986; Taylor, 2016), Acemoglu and Robinson's (2012) theory on inclusive and extractive institutions, and participatory governance theory (Fischer, 2016; Fung, 2006, 2015; Fung and Wright, 2003). All three strands of thinking aid our understanding of government as an institution, questioning whether governance in the form of elected representative democracy is the best way of solving complex problems in the modern world. Its institutional failure breaks down society's resilience, prosperity and dynamism.

SOCIAL COORDINATION: HOW DO WE DO STUFF TOGETHER?

Whenever we discuss any kind of policy, we are ultimately trying to figure out how to solve complex problems – as leaders, as communities and as individuals. Each of these three actors has their strengths and their weaknesses. Arguably, humans flourish and work best when there is an equilibrium between them and the inevitable tensions that arise between hierarchical, solidaristic and individual-istic forms of problem-solving are managed.

As Matthew Taylor (2016) has eloquently argued, for institutions to have a high degree of creativity and individual autonomy, they need a combination of hierarchical, solidaristic and individualistic elements. Charlie Leadbeater aptly calls this "creative communities with a cause" (2014). Both refer to the human role in solving collec-tive dilemmas and the need to balance hierarchical, solidaristic and individualistic tendencies.

The hierarchical view emphasises leadership, strategy and exper-tise. Ideally, it has a clear and consistent vision and strategy, it trusts and empowers and it is directed at ends and values (it has purpose). The solidaristic perspective stresses the importance of solidarity and belonging, the sharing of norms, identity and values. This can tend one of two ways – a 'solidarity for' or a 'solidarity against' which can be either expansive or exclusive. Leadbeater's notion of community clearly stresses the former. Finally, the individualistic standpoint sees coordination as spontaneous; the aim is to provide a platform for competition and ambition to flourish. The ideal form is one of empowerment – of others as well as the self. Taken together, one can imagine a government that exhibits value-based leader-ship, encourages inclusive and constructive solidarity, and a model of engaged individualism which promotes personal growth and empowers citizens to create the lives they choose.

Yet our democratic institutions today leave us far from call-ing ourselves a "creative community with a cause". The presence and popularity of populist parties points to democratic fatigue and fragmentation – symptoms of institutional weakening (Chwalisz, 2015). Not limited to the UK or even to Europe, we have witnessed this phenomenon across the globe. Donald Trump winning the presidential election. The populist Five Star Movement gaining new footholds of local support in Italy, winning power in key cities such as Rome. New political parties on the populist left – Podemos – and the centre – Ciudadanos – causing political deadlock in Spain, leaving the country without a government for close to a year. The

Icelandic Pirate party winning the most votes in the October 2016 elections following the Panama Papers tax evasion scandal. The far-right Alternative for Germany party coming second in Angela Merkel's constituency in regional elections, pushing her Christian Democrats into third place in 2016. Austria was within less than a percentage point of electing a far-right president – an election that was contested a second time with the outcome that was still relatively close run. Hungary and Poland both have populist leaders in positions of power. As do India and Turkey, with Narendra Modi and Recep Tayyip Erdoğan positioning themselves as populist strongmen.

The institutional challenges our democracies are facing, however, are not necessarily the fault of the people, the politicians or even the parties. The blunt tools of elections and referendums fuel a divisive, adversarial form of politics on one hand, and perpetuate the dominance of what seems to be an elected aristocracy on the other (see 'Elitist Britain,' 2014). The result is an understandable feeling of wanting to regain 'control'.

However, taking the UK's referendum on EU membership as an example, it is precisely the type of complex issue that might have better lent itself to some form of deliberative democracy. Political leaders would set the remit for a group of representative citizens, selected through a robust and transparent procedure, to spend numerous months examining the evidence, hearing from leading experts, and deliberating with one another to propose recommendations for action. Overseen by trained and impartial facilitators, the proceedings would be open for the public to follow, while allowing them access to all of the same information. The citizens taking part in the process could also hear evidence from their fellow citizens. Citizens' collective recommendations, decided by weighing the trade-offs and reaching conclusions by consensus, would be influential, but advisory. The process would seek to unite societies in their search for common ground, rather than divide them. It would complement, not overwhelm, the institutions of representative democracy.

INCLUSIVE INSTITUTIONS

Representative democratic institutions have been evolving in western Europe and around the world slowly and gradually. In Britain, the 1831 general election was mostly about the single issue of political reform. Soon after, in 1838, the Chartist Movement led the campaign for universal suffrage for men, arguing that it was the only way to empower the masses. After successive failures to pressure the government into reforms beyond those made in 1832, the Chartist Movement disintegrated, and was followed by the National Reform Union and the Reform League 30 years later. Only after pro-reform riots in Hyde Park in 1866 was the Second Reform Act passed the following year, doubling the size of the electorate. Soon after, the secret ballot was introduced and other corrupt electoral practices, such as bribery, were prohibited. Twenty years later, the Third Reform Act of 1884 increased the size of the electorate again – to 60% of adult males. In 1918, the Representation of the People Act gave the vote to all adult males over 21 and to all women over 30 who were taxpayers or were married to taxpayers. One decade later, women gained the same rights as men. Political reform towards more inclusive institutions was a slow and arduous process.

But it went hand in hand with the growth of more inclusive economic institutions, which Acemoglu and Robinson (2012) argue are the driver of national prosperity. For instance, over this same period of struggle for political rights, the education system gradually changed from being primarily run for the elite to being accessible to the masses. The civil service was opened up to public examination, making it more meritocratic. And various pieces of legislation such as the Masters and Servants Acts, which permitted employers to use the law to limit the mobility of their workers, were repealed to tilt the balance of power in favour of workers. It was a "virtuous circle of inclusive institutions" (Acemoglu and Robinson, 2012).

Furthermore, a growing body of research highlights the positive association between citizen engagement in rulemaking and economic prosperity (Johns and Saltane, 2016; OECD, 2009; Gurin, 2014). Numerous studies emphasise that it is not a government's openness to integrating modern communications technology which is important, but rather its responsiveness to its citizens (Yu and Robinson, 2012). An ambitious World Bank paper by Johns and Saltane (2016) examines citizen engagement in rulemaking in 185 countries, arguing that greater citizen involvement is associated with higher-quality regulation, stronger democratic regimes and less corrupt institutions. The authors develop a composite score based on six factors: publication of proposed regulations; consultation on proposed regulations; reporting back on results of consultations; conducting regulatory impact assessments; presence of a specialised body to review impact assessments; and publication of regulatory impact assessments. Canada and Australia are two of the only countries to receive a perfect six out of six score. The UK ranks highly, but loses points for "consultation on proposed regulations" and "reporting back on results of consultations". Of course, regulations are but one type of policy area, but the study nonetheless sheds important light on the quality of citizen engagement in policymaking and the economic and democratic consequences.

PARTICIPATORY GOVERNANCE

Finally, the large body of literature on participatory governance has been equally influential. Defined as a "variant or subset of governance theory that puts emphasis on democratic engagement, in particular through deliberative practices" (Fischer, 2016), participatory governance refers to the developments in political theory about deliberative democracy, as well as the deliberative experiments on the part of various public organisations. The case studies from Canada and Australia discussed in the following chapter fall neatly into the latter category. From this perspective, citizens' roles are not confined to being voters or watchdogs, rather as active participants through direct deliberative engagement on the pressing problems of our time. Fung and Wright (2003) refer to it as "empowered participatory governance", stressing that the process of engaging citizens in "reason-based action-oriented decision-making" offers a radical political step towards a more democratic society (*ibid*). Defining participatory governance is key for this study as it leads to a reconceptualisation of the role of politicians and public servants today as facilitators of public engagement.

The benefits of political leaders and civil servants engaging in participatory governance are well documented. Across fields as diverse as education, health care, infrastructure development and environmental protection among others, an approach which engages citizens directly in the decision-making process leads to faster responses to problems, more effective design and development of appropriate solutions, and higher levels of commitment and motivation to implement the programme. Importantly, there are also higher levels of public satisfaction with policies that have been developed in a participatory way (Fischer, 2016).

It is in this sense that long-form deliberative processes are discussed throughout this book in terms of both their democratic qualities and their ability to promote more effective governance. New inclusive democratic institutions can help governments to gain public trust and legitimacy by adding an informed public voice to the public decision-making process. In doing so, they are able to inspire confidence and get past political gridlock to develop more effective, long-term policies. For we face difficult challenges: housing shortages, chronically low productivity, inadequate infrastructure, climate change, falling living standards and high youth unemployment, among others. If we are to tackle them in order to build a more prosperous future, our democratic institutions will need to be renewed.

METHODOLOGY

To try and understand whether long-form deliberative processes have a key role to play in invigorating our democratic institutions, this research explores their extensive use in Canada and Australia. These two Commonwealth nations have been pioneering the use of long-form deliberative processes for close to a decade. At the time of writing, and to the extent of my knowledge, these are the only examples where this specific, rigorous method has been used consistently over many years, and for a diverse range of issues. It is partly for these reasons that they were chosen for comparison. Of course, Canada and Australia are both more federal in character than the UK. However, it is thought that with regional devolution in England on the political agenda, it is the appropriate moment to consider how British political leaders could reinvent their public engagement methods.

The case studies in this book were first compiled on the basis of extensive online research, thanks in part to the fact that most of the examples have been conducted by three organisations – MASS LBP and the Centre for Public Involvement in Canada and the newDemocracy Foundation in Australia. This was complemented by over 30 semi-structured face-to-face and telephone interviews with the organisations' founders, directors and staff members, as well as various government authorities who commissioned the long-form deliberative processes – premiers, ministers, engagement leads and numerous civil servants.

These were also supplemented by less formal interviews with academics, thinktank fellows, and former civil servants and political advisers, who were not necessarily directly involved with any of the case studies in this publication, but who have either a deep knowledge of or involvement with earlier cases (such as the large-scale citizens' assemblies on electoral reform in British Columbia and Ontario), or extensive expertise in deliberative theory or policy formation.

In addition to the interviews, the analysis also relies on a categorisation of all of the cases on the basis of their level of governance, duration, method, outcome and cost in order to gauge their effectiveness, to develop a set of success factors and to clarify the types of policy dilemma that can be resolved through long-form deliberations.

Finally, as this is a comparative analysis, the Canadian and Australian case studies are considered in relation to the closest British equivalents: traditional consultation processes such as royal commissions and inquiries, as well as the experiments with citizens' juries in the New Labour years and more recent academic trials. A combination of desk research, primarily reliant on the National Archives, interviews with former political advisers to the New Labour government and with the academics and organisers of the recent citizens' juries, as well as attendance at one of the citizens' assembly pilots in Southampton, inform this element of the study.

BETTER TOGETHER

Learning from best practice in Canada and Australia

While they are thousands of miles apart, Canada and Australia share much in common when it comes to reinventing public consultation. In both countries, and completely separate of one another, the democratic innovation has largely been led by an independent company or organisation that has specialised predominantly in long-form deliberative processes. In Canada, they are often called citizens' reference panels. In Australia, the preferred term is citizens' juries. But beyond the semantic divergence, the methodology and the principles behind them are the same. Since 2010, there are close to 50 cases – roughly evenly split between the countries – to examine. It is mainly for these reasons that they were chosen as points of comparison and of reference for the UK.

Of course, despite the parallels, no two countries are identical and there are some differences worth noting. Canada and Australia are markedly more federal, with much greater power devolved to both provincial/state and city levels. It means that there is already a greater appreciation and understanding of shared public decisions. Equally, it indicates that important choices, such as big infrastructure investments, long-term energy generation questions and billion-dollar budgets also get decided at a level of government which is one step closer to the citizen. The UK remains one of the Organisation for Economic Co-operation and Development's most centralised countries. The devolution which has taken place has been sporadic and irregularly distributed, notably with the Scottish parliament, Welsh assembly and the London mayoralty each having differing powers, as well as more rights than those given to the English regions and cities. However, this need not be seen solely as a negative, as the 'northern powerhouse' and new 'city deals' currently on the agenda present a unique opportunity for establishing democratic institutions for public decision-making at these new levels of governance from the outset.

In this section, five in-depth case studies will be discussed from each country – long-form deliberative processes that have taken place at various levels of governance, on a wide range of topics, and to varying levels of success when it comes to the aim of creating effective and legitimate policies with public support. In doing so, the design characteristics and key factors that define a rigorous and transparent public consultation can be emphasised.

It is also worth highlighting at this point a number of features which are common to most cases featured in this study:

• **Random selection process**: often around 10,000 random invitations to participate are sent by post, with a 5–12% response rate, meaning around 500 to 1,200 people respond. Among respondents, a random sample is chosen, stratifying for age, gender and usually one or two other criteria such as housing tenure or geography, both of which tend to be correlated with other socio-economic indicators such as income level and education.
• **Trustee role**: participants are not asked to think about issues from their own personal point of view, but more broadly as citizens of a wider community.
• **Time**: participants have the opportunity to learn and to meet with one another for two to three months, coming together in person between four to six times. The process is broken down

into separate learning, understanding, deliberating and proposing stages.

- **Authority**: the public authority commissioning the long-form deliberative process agrees to publicly and directly respond to (not necessarily accept) all of the recommendations.
- **Publicity**: it is a public process. Early on, there is a commitment to promote the long-form deliberation in the press before any recommendations are made. It helps to engage the wider community and to build trust in the jury or panel members, and thus also the outcome.

CASE STUDIES: KEY FIGURES

The following tables provide an overview of the key characteristics of long-form deliberative processes in Canada and Australia, the level of governance at which they have taken place, and a summary of the types of issues for which they have been used.

Table 1. Overview of long-form deliberative processes in Canada and Australia from 2010–16

Average	
Duration	Five full-day, in-person meetings over three months
Number of participants	38
Number of invitations posted	9,200
Cost	$161,000

Table 2. Level of governance in long-form deliberative processes in Canada and Australia from 2010–16

Level	Number of occurrences
National	2
State/provincial	11
Regional	5
City	30

Table 3. Issues covered in long-form deliberative processes in Canada and Australia from 2010–16

Topic	Number of occurrences
Public health	10
Infrastructure investment	7
Strategic city plan	7
Local issues	7
Planning/housing	5
Political institutions	4
Energy	2
Arts/culture	2
Environment	2
Digital services	1
Cycling infrastructure	1
Agriculture	1

CANADA

Table 4. Overview of long-form deliberative processes in Canada

Average	
Duration	Five full-day, in-person meetings over two to three months
Number of participants	36
Number of invitations posted	9,940

The Canadian examples discussed in detail are as follows. All of the other cases are listed and briefly described in the appendix. The following examples were chosen for in-depth discussion as they have taken place at various levels of governance and are all on different topics, illustrating the breadth of possibilities that these processes can be used for, while at the same time highlighting the unifying characteristics between them.

I. Residents' Panel on the Ontario Condominium Act 2012

The Residents' Panel on the Ontario Condominium Act remains one of the best examples of citizen engagement in policymaking which directly influenced legislative change. While not solely responsible, the voices of condominium owners and dwellers played a key part

Table 5. Overview of in-depth Canadian case studies

Level of governance	Topic	Duration	No. of invitations	No. of participants	Cost (CAD)
Provincial	Residents' Panel on the Ontario Condominium Act 2012	Three full-day meetings over two months, one full-day follow-up meeting a year later	10,000	36	$122,000
Regional	Metrolinx: Residents' Reference Panel on Regional Transportation Investment 2013	Four full-day meetings over two months	10,000	36	$135,000
Provincial	British Columbia Services Card User Panel 2013	Four full-day meetings, plus two evenings over one month	16,500	36	$216,400
National	Canada Mental Health Action Plan 2015 Citizens' Reference Panel 2015	Five full-day meetings in a row	10,000	36	$204,000
City	Toronto Planning Review Panel 2016-18	16 meetings over 2.5 years (ongoing)	12,000	28	$100,000

in the government's public consultation process alongside open submissions from the wider public and stakeholder meetings.

The Canadian province of Ontario is at the heart of North America's condominium boom. Around 1.3 million – 10% of Ontario's 13.6 million population – live in condominiums. But the legislation governing condo living was outdated, passed in 1998 and last updated in 2001. Moreover, privately owned apartments have increasingly become the first choice of new buyers and retirees.

To update the Condominium Act, the Ontario Ministry of Government and Consumer Services developed a four-track engagement process: the residents' panel run by MASS LBP; complementary information sessions and town hall meetings; stakeholder roundtables; and public submissions. During the first stage, the public brought issues to the table through each of these four streams. The second stage involved a panel of experts reviewing and fleshing out the findings. The final stage involved a follow-up meeting with members of the residents' panel to review the solutions report; an opportunity both to demonstrate that their ideas had been taken on board, and to allow for last comments and advice. Although the town hall meetings and public submissions were important, the residents' panel and the technical stakeholder group had the most important impact on the outcome.

The role of the residents' panel in this four-tier engagement process was particularly important, as it allowed condominium owners and dwellers to develop and promote a collective voice rather than offering simply individual points of view. According to the former deputy minister of government and consumer services, Giles Gherson:

"The residents' panel was necessary to ensure that condo residents could develop a structured and sophisticated viewpoint on the several different elements of the review – some quite technical – so that their voice would carry equal weight and contribute on an equal footing with more experienced, established stakeholder groups that were part of the public engagement table. That's why we convened the residents' panel as a separate exercise. With the culmination of their report, we invited members to join the public engagement table where they could represent and advocate for the residents' panel consensus".

Initially, there was some scepticism from the premier's office about the panel; it was concerned that any condominium act reform process might lead to a set of costly regulatory measures that would need to be paid for by condo owners, but for which the government would be held responsible. Eventually, with backing from the sector, developers and residents for the outcomes of the public engagement process, the government supported the idea of modest fees to pay for a new body to oversee the implementation of the reforms. As with the Toronto planning review panel, the 36 panellists were chosen by a two-stage random selection process called a civic lottery. Ten thousand official letters from Gherson invited people to represent the condominium community's views as part of the residents' panel. Invitations were randomly sent to condominium residences across the province and were transferable to anyone over the age of 18 who lived in the same condo corporation. Each region of Ontario received a number of invitations proportionate to its population. Condominium developers and managers, elected political representatives and employees of the government ministry were ineligible to participate.

Over 500 people responded, either volunteering to be part of the panel or asking to remain informed about the process. The final 36 participants were chosen randomly from this pool, stratifying for gender, age, geographical distribution, type of condominium residence and whether the individual rented or owned the apartment. The final panel consisted mainly of residents who owned their condominium, with six renters and six landlords also selected. Panellists were not paid, but all of their expenses were covered.

Meeting three times over two months in October and November 2012, the panel learned about the legislation, identified trade-offs and priorities and proposed directions and options for amending and improving the Condominium Act.

At their first meeting, the panellists were welcomed by the minister of consumer services. "At first", recalls Phil Simeon, the residents' panel manager, "the participants were not entirely sure why they were there. They were expecting an old school consultation, wondering if their voice really mattered". The MASS LBP team explained the process and the learning phase began. Participants received an overview of condos in their province, heard presentations, and asked questions of a range of experts, people working within the ministry and stakeholders from organisations such as the

Canada Mortgage and Housing Corporation and the Ontario Home
Builders' Association. Working with a facilitator, they also established the values which they wanted to guide their discussions for
modernising the legislation.

After a two-week break, the group reconvened. During that time,
they had been asked to do some background reading. Additionally,
they were to speak with at least five friends, family members or
neighbours about the discussions and presentations from the first
meeting and elicit feedback about the priorities for change. In all,
the 36 panellists collectively consulted 314 other condo residents
during that time, almost double the number they were asked to speak
to. The start of their second meeting concluded the 'learning phase'
with two additional 'conversations' with guest experts.

The next stage then commenced, as panellists worked in small
groups to write out on small cards all of the concerns that they had
become aware of. These were then sorted into six categories: consumer protection for buyers; condominium manager qualifications;
condominium governance; financial management; dispute resolu-
tion; and an 'other' category. Choosing the issue area they were
most interested in, panellists split into six groups to flesh them out.
By the end of the day, they were able to organise all of the cards into
concrete issues and begin to draft their section of recommendations
for the panel report.

During another two-week break, they were provided with a version of all of the panel's collective work, which had been typed up
by the MASS LBP team. The panellists examined the draft, revising
certain sections, noting anything missing or ambiguities to deliberate on further before reconvening for a third full day to draft their
final report.

This last session began in small groups related to the six issues
from the previous meeting. Each table had a large paper template to
fill in, which gave the issue a title, premise and values statements,
recommended concrete suggestions of what could be done and how
it would be funded, and a desired outcome statement of what success
might look like. Presentations from each group back to the rest of

the residents' panel resulted in constructive feedback and revisions in the afternoon. Refining their sections, they eventually arrived at a version that was approved by all 36 members and bound into the Draft Report of the Residents' Panel to Review the Condominium Act. At the end of the day, each chapter was read aloud by someone from each issues group at a podium to Gherson.

Reflecting on the panel's contribution, Gherson said he was "very impressed by the quality of recommendations and the commitment of the participants. It was interesting to see what concerned them". A research report by Don Lenihan for the Public Policy Forum (2014) found that stakeholders were very respectful of the residents' panel recommendations, returning to the report "over and over again".

The residents' recommendations were fed into the considerations of a panel of experts who were asked by the ministry to develop a solutions report. Nearly one year later, the residents' panel was reconvened in September 2013 to review and comment on the solutions report before it was finalised. After assessing more than 100 recommendations that were part of the report, the panel's overall conclusion was that the proposals effectively responded to a large majority of their priorities and concerns. Gherson confirmed that "the citizens' reference panel was taken seriously. A large number of their recommendations made it into the condo act". The process was highly praised, inspiring other Ontario ministries to use public engagement as a key element of the policymaking process.

2. Metrolinx: Residents' Reference Panel on Regional Transportation Investment 2013

Metrolinx is an agency of the government of Ontario which coordinates and integrates all modes of transport in the Greater Toronto and Hamilton Area (GTHA). They have worked twice with MASS LBP to organise citizens' reference panels to make important and difficult decisions about transport infrastructure. The Residents' Reference Panel on Regional Transportation Investment in 2013 was one part of a three-tier engagement strategy, alongside a 'conversation kit' distributed to the wider public and 16 roundtable meetings across the region.

Through a two-tier civic lottery, 10,000 people were randomly invited to participate. Letters were sent out across the GTHA, with each part receiving a number proportionate to its population. Among the 410 who responded, a stratified group of 36 panellists was chosen, representative of age, gender, and population distribution in the region based on 2011 data. There was no special selection according to ethnicity, income, educational attainment or other attributes, but this emerged proportionally due to the random selection element. As with all of MASS LBP's reference panels, the participants were not paid, but their expenses were covered.

The residents' reference panel met over the course of four Saturdays in February and March 2013. Its purpose was to learn about the existing transit systems in the GTHA, proposed additions, other transport systems around the world, the variety of funding options available for transit investment and the transport needs for the region. The panel's remit was "to propose recommendations to inform Metrolinx's strategy for raising funds to make long-term, sustainable investments in transit and transportation in the GTHA" (MASS LBP for Metrolinx, 2013).

Following the same process of learning, deliberation and recommendations, the panel's first day began with a welcome from the president and CEO of Metrolinx, followed by presentations involving eight different participants, including senior Metrolinx staff, independent experts and representatives from some of the region's transit authorities. During a question and answer period, policymakers, and transit operators answered questions about the economy and the population of the GTHA, about provincial and local transport policy decisions and the lessons to be learnt from other regions. Panellists then wrote down their "vision for transportation in the GTHA" – their ideal proposition – and discussed it in small groups. At the end of the day, they were given a conversation kit and asked to review it and speak with friends and family before the next meeting.

Reconvening one week later, the second deliberative meeting continued the learning phase. Metrolinx's president and CEO presented the group with the currently unfunded projects to be completed before 2031. The idea of cost-benefit analysis was also explained. In this context, small groups discussed once again their "vision for transportation in the GTHA" and whether it could be achieved. Later on in the day, they listened to Metrolinx staff on the work they had done to date to identify 26 potential revenue-raising methods – taxes and user fees – to fund its investment strategy, as well as presentations by various stakeholders, industry representatives and academics. The panel then discussed which principles should guide their deliberations about solutions and proposals, deciding that funding principles should be used to evaluate the various revenue-generating options available, and to combine these into funding scenarios that could raise adequate funds for their ideas. At the end of the second meeting ahead of the deliberating phase, the panellists were reminded that their task was not to develop a personal position, but rather a rationale for their views and to engage with others in order to find common ground. Their task ahead of the next meeting was to review a booklet of 26 different revenue-raising measures used in other jurisdictions.

Day three began with panellists sharing details of the conversations they had had during the week with their friends and family, along with any questions that had occurred to them over that time. They worked in small groups on different funding principles, drafting short statements about why their chosen principles were important. These were then shared with the rest of the room. Panellists then split into groups of two to work on the 26 funding ideas, considering their benefits and drawbacks. They gave one-minute presentations back to the whole group listing the most persuasive points for and against each measure. After a presentation on how to give strong policy recommendations, panellists began drafting funding scenarios. They started with a blank sheet which had an empty 'thermometer' on it, broken down by increments marked between zero and $2bn CAD. Each group received cut-outs with all of the revenue measures, sized according to how much money they would bring in annually and colour-coded based on who would bear the cost (user, beneficiary, or everyone).

On the final day, the small groups reunited to continue their work from the previous meeting. They began by reviewing what they had done thus far – the funding principles and the funding scenarios. They filled in large template sheets which would inform the final report, naming their scenario, listing the selected revenue measures, explaining why they were chosen, and providing a rationale for the mix of measures. Each group presented to their fellow panellists, who, in turn, reacted to their ideas, provided feedback and asked questions. After a final session to revise their propositions, and for a small break-away group to draft a section about the panel's vision for the GTHA's transport system and its funding principles, they had one last feedback round. At the end of the day, all drafts were collected and collated to form the Draft Report from the Residents' Reference Panel. A representative from each of the small groups orally presented their section of the draft to the president and CEO of Metrolinx. The report was then passed on, following an editing process involving the panellists, to the Metrolinx staff and board of directors.

Some of the panel's recommendations included:

• Metrolinx should propose a one percentage point increase to the Harmonized Sales Tax (equivalent to VAT in the UK), raising over two-thirds of the $2bn CAD needed annually to fund The Big Move (the regional transport plan).
• The balance should be raised by increasing corporate income tax and added fees aimed at drivers – either a top-up to the provincial vehicle registration fee, a 1.5% increase in provincial fuel tax or a parking levy.
• The federal government also has a role to play in long-term funding of major infrastructure projects.
• New revenues should be dedicated to transport infrastructure and not to be used for other purposes.

The Metrolinx board and management considered the panel's recommendations, with the board accepting the management's recommendations, which matched most of the panel's proposals (with the omission of the corporate tax proposal plus a number of additional funding options). They thus took on the following recommendations:

- One percent increase in HST, but with a mobility tax credit so as not to disproportionately burden those on lower incomes.
- Regional fuel and gas tax – five cents per litre, business parking levy, development charges.
- All funds placed in a dedicated trust to fund The Big Move investment projects, which would not be used for other purposes.

Judy Pfeifer, chief communications and public affairs officer at Metrolinx, was the internal advocate for the process over other forms of public consultation. In an interview in February 2016, she explained: "At first I was sceptical about how representative it would be – but it was. But it was clear that the participants really wanted to make their community better. People were really thoughtful deliberators".

As to why Metrolinx chose long-form deliberation as its form of public consultation, Pfeifer said she is "not convinced by the representativeness of town hall meetings. While it still needs to happen I am not sure it can be our main engagement tool. We are looking rather towards citizens' juries and digital engagement". This explains why Metrolinx has done two reference panels on different topics, both run by MASS LBP thus far, and why Pfeifer says that they will probably do more in the future.

3. British Columbia Services Card User Panel 2013

In 2013, the British Columbia (BC) Ministry of Technology, Innovation and Citizens' Services held a digital service consultation to address security and privacy concerns about the introduction of a new services card – a security-enhanced photo ID with an encrypted chip used to access more government services online. The lead initiative of the consultation was a user panel with a group of 35 randomly selected citizens, representative of BC residents, which was run by MASS LBP. The consultation was also complemented by a specialist forum, which gathered the perspectives of industry leaders, stakeholders and academics, and an online survey targeted at the general public.

Through MASS LBP's characteristic civic lottery process, 16,500 households across the province received an invitation to participate in the user panel from Andrew Wilkinson, minister of technology, innovation and citizens' services. More than 725 people responded, of which 35 were randomly selected to become panellists, controlling for gender, age and geographic distribution. At least one place was reserved for an Aboriginal resident and another for a person with a disability. The users' panel volunteered over 40 hours of their time, without getting paid (but their expenses were covered).

The panel's purpose was to learn about the BC services card and the identity management system that will make it possible to secure online access to government services. Its remit was to provide direction to the government concerning panellists' values and priorities with regard to digital identity card services and propose recommendations to increase public confidence in the services card.

Over two weekends in November and December 2013, the panellists went through the same learning, deliberation and recommendations process common to the other case studies. Given the size of British Columbia and the fact that participants had travelled from across the province to participate, each set of meetings took place over the entirety of a weekend rather than one-day meetings spread over a longer duration of time.

The evening prior to their first weekend, the panel met for the first time over dinner. They were welcomed by MASS LBP's principal, Peter MacLeod, who also gave an overview of the process. The panellists also heard their first presentation from Professor Colin Bennett, an expert on national identity systems and cards. He gave them five questions to keep in mind over the course of the two weekends:

- Is the type of authentication appropriately matched to the problem that needs solving?
- Are there simpler, less risky solutions to the problem being described?
- What is going on beneath the surface of the services card programme?
- How is data analysed and stored?
- What are the implications for offline access if online services become widely popular?

After a question and answer session, the evening concluded ahead of the weekend's activities. On the first morning, the panellists were greeted by Andrew Wilkinson, the minister who had invited them to attend. Following a recap about how the process works, they discussed why they had wanted to attend the panel, and broke into small groups to discuss the various forms of identification they used on an everyday basis. The rest of the day contained presentations from government representatives, internet entrepreneurs, digital identity and security experts, and civil liberty campaigners. After a break and dinner, the group reconvened to hear from three more experts: a manager in Driver Licensing, the executive director of the BC Freedom of Information and Privacy Association, and the chair of the Digital Identity and Authentication Council of Canada/deputy minister of the BC Ministry of Energy and Mines.

On the second day, the deliberation phase began. The panellists spent the morning discussing and prioritising the government services which they use most frequently, those they would want to be able to access online and whether it would make them uncomfortable to use the services card to access any of them. They listed all of the services on a spectrum from 'not at all' to 'completely' comfortable. Towards the end of the day, the group also established the values which are important in relation to online services, which they would keep in mind the following weekend.

The user panel's next meeting began the following Friday evening over dinner. Once again, their meal was followed by another presentation, this time from the executive director for the legislation, privacy and policy branch within the office of BC's chief information officer, who outlined the protections that are part of the province's Freedom of Information and Protection of Privacy Act, the role that the information and privacy commissioner plays, and how the act is regularly amended to keep up to date with technological advances.

The next day, the panellists began by reviewing the government's online public survey on digital services and the BC services card and learned about the 14 key privacy and security commitments that the government had made. They reviewed the values which they had established were important for designing online services at the end of the previous weekend, and heard from one last speaker, BC's information and privacy commissioner. The panel split into smaller groups, each relating to one of seven areas of government services: health; transport; income support and social services; education and libraries; business, licences and taxes; and miscellaneous services (including citizenship and payment, for example). Considering the benefits and risks of using the services card, they sorted the services within their group into: provisionally acceptable uses, additional caution recommended, and restricted uses. They presented their key arguments to the rest of the group, getting feedback and comments from their peers before turning their focus to the actions that government could take to increase confidence in the services card's digital authentication features. Again, the small groups presented back to the wider panel and asked for constructive feedback. They found that some of their ideas were specific to their services, while others were universal and recurred in the presentations of other groups.

On the final day, the users' panel focused on the recommendations stage, working to get their ideas into a concrete draft they could present by the end of the afternoon. The panel's chair gave them a few tips for structuring their recommendations. Over half of the panellists remained within the services-themed groups, while others split to form new teams which concentrated on drafting: the introduction, the guiding values for digital services and for identity management systems, and the 'universal confidence measures'. A few hours later, the groups presented, gathered feedback and asked questions to each other, flagging any outstanding issues or strong objections. A number of recommendations were dropped or seriously revised at this stage, highlighting the benefits of such a process in helping a diverse group of individuals to reach a consensus. Once the users' panel agreed on their final proposals, panellists presented the individual sections to John Jacobson, the deputy minister of technology, innovation and citizens' services.

The panel proposed 10 recommendations for additional measures before the digital authentication is activated. A few months later, Andrew Wilkinson directly responded to each proposal in a report, accepting all of them and explaining how they will be met (British Columbia Ministry of Technology, Innovation and Citizens' Services, 2014). As the minister wrote in the report's introduction, the efforts of the users' panel "provided invaluable feedback that will help light the way forward for [the government's] digital services strategy". The report also mentioned the principles that were developed by the users' panel for guiding the government's approach to online services.

4. Canada Mental Health Action Plan Citizens' Reference Panel 2015

In June 2015, the first-ever national citizens' reference panel took place to inform the Mental Health Commission of Canada's priorities. The Mental Health Commission is a national registered non-profit, funded by the federal government. Over the course of four years, experts had put together a Mental Health Action Plan, outlining visions, values and goals, but no priorities. The plan was devised based upon a province-by-province tour which engaged with a self-selecting group of contributors, as well as a national online survey, which had a 30% response rate among the 25,000 approached. Most of the respondents, however, had personal experience of the issues

involved and their answers reflected those experiences. The commission thus wanted to hold a citizens' reference panel to overcome
the difficulty of always talking to the same people rather than a
cross-section of the public.

Organised and run by MASS LBP, the Canada Mental Health
Action Plan Citizens' Reference Panel was composed of a diverse
group of 36 Canadians from across the country, chosen once again
through a civic lottery. Ten thousand households across the country
received a letter from Louise Bradley, the president and CEO of
the Mental Health Commission of Canada, inviting them to participate as panellists. More than 510 people responded, of whom
36 were selected, controlling for gender, age, geography, language
preference (as it was a bilingual panel), and ensuring proportionate
representation of Aboriginal people and visible minorities. Due to
Canada's vast size and travel distances required (the majority of its
costs were travel-related), the panel was convened over the course
of five full days at the National Arts Centre in Ottawa.

During this time, they went through a series of stages akin to
those in other case studies: learning, deliberation and recommendations. Together, MASS LBP and the commission partnered on
who to invite as experts and traditional stakeholders were asked
to observe. The panellists heard from 20 experts, deepening their
knowledge about mental health in Canada through a combination
of statistics and stories from those working within the mental health
system. They were informed about different types of mental illness,
the demographics of mental health and the variety of services available, from prevention to treatments. Panellists learned about the
needs of different groups, including young people, new immigrants,
Aboriginal people, those who have experienced homelessness, and
others. They heard presentations about research efforts as well as
research gaps.

The learning phase of the panel ended with a dinner with people
who had experienced mental illness, including various public per-
sonalities such as radio hosts, who shared personal stories about a
wide range of conditions, including postnatal depression, bipolar

disorder, post-traumatic stress disorder, psychosis and schizo-phrenia. Speaking about the challenges and stigma they faced, as well as their road to recovery, the conversations were moving and "continued well into the evening, with many members remaining to have one-on-one conversations with guests long after the evening was officially brought to a close" (Mental Health Commission of Canada, 2016).

Reflecting on what they had learnt, the panellists began the delib-eration phase, working in six small groups. Helped by a facilitator, they sought to identify the principles which they wanted the Mental Health Action Plan to reflect. They identified six of them, decid-ing that the plan should be: client-centred, adaptable, effective, evidence-based and measurable, holistic, and realistic. Continuing to work in small groups, the panellists mapped out all of the actors and stakeholders in the field of mental health to help keep in mind those who would benefit and those they should target with their recommendations.

Once this was established, the panel reviewed the Mental Health Action Plan for Canada's 109 recommendations. Each of the six groups received a pack of 109 cards with all of the recommendations and discussed which of the recommendations should be prioritised and which should be put to one side for the next five years. They then reorganised themselves into six new working groups, each one focused on one of the 'strategic directions' identified in the strategy. They examined the recommendations which fell under their remit and whether any were missing, narrowing their strategic direction down to no more than six recommendations by recombining, rewrit-ing, removing and adding content. The small groups shared their recommendations with the whole group, receiving feedback and comments to refine their propositions.

On the final day, the panel surveyed its collective efforts, highlight-ing themes that cut across the various strategic directions and identi-fying them as the foundations of their recommendations. These were: 'the social determinants of health'; 'early detection and treatment'; 'community capacity'; and 'reaching a tipping point and increasing

funding'. Working in five groups, they fleshed out these themes and
worked on an introductory preamble to add to their report.

At the end of the five days, the panellists presented their final
report with 18 recommendations – written in their own words –
to the commission's president and CEO as well as the chair and
vice-chair of the commission's board, Canada's former minister of
finance, Michael Wilson. Panellists took turns to present their report
orally. Their presentation was filmed, shared with those who were
not able to attend in person and screened at the commission's next
board meeting. A minority report was attached to the panel's recommendations, featuring a number of views which were not agreed by
consensus in the group, but which panellists wanted included in the
final document.

The reference panel's report was not made public immediately
due to a moratorium imposed by the sudden election called by the
then prime minister Stephen Harper in the summer of 2015. While
this caused a degree of frustration for the panellists and some
people working within the commission, MASS LBP's principal
Peter MacLeod said the citizens' report was nonetheless influential
in shaping the commission's internal thinking. One year later, the
citizens' reference panel report, with its 18 recommendations, was
published by the Mental Health Commission, and forms the corner-
stone of its Mental Health Action Plan for Canada.

This example highlights the benefits and possibility of using a
rigorous deliberative process, involving ordinary citizens, to solve
important public problems at the national level. The University of
British Columbia Centre for Health Services and Policy, funded by
the Canadian Institutes of Health Research, held a national citizens'
reference panel on pharmacare in October 2016 over a four-day
period. Its purpose was to review provincial and federal policies
concerning drug coverage and consider whether different models
would better suit the needs of Canadians. The remit was to issue
a public report with its recommendations shared with the federal
health minister and her provincial and territorial counterparts. If it is
possible and effective to organise such panels in a country the size of

Canada, it shows the possibility of making a long-form deliberative process work at various scales. The issue is not necessarily the level of governance, but rather the salience of the topic and the nature of the problem that needs to be solved.

5. Toronto Planning Review Panel 2016–18

As an ongoing project, the Toronto Planning Review Panel cannot be examined in the same way as the other case studies. However, due to its ambitious aims and unique format, it is worth highlighting in this book. Unlike the other examples, it extends beyond the definition of long-form deliberative processes, which are typically characterised as involving a randomly selected group of up to 50 citizens who meet around four to six times over two to three months to deliberate about and advise on a specific policy matter. Rather, 28 randomly selected Torontonians have volunteered their time and effort for over two years to deliberate on a variety of planning questions. After four full-day training sessions, they are meeting once every two months for two years.

The panel's mandate is: "To provide input on city planning strategies, plans, politics, and initiatives that have city-wide implications. This input should be provided in order to help ensure city planning's activities are informed by resident experience and well-aligned with the values and priorities of all Torontonians. To achieve their mandate, panellists are tasked to:

- Learn about Toronto, the ways the city is changing, and the different roles that city planning plays in guiding growth and change;
- Understand the different values, perspectives, experiences, and priorities of all Toronto residents and commuters – including those who are vulnerable, marginalised, or homeless – concerning their local neighbourhoods and the city as a whole; and
- Work together to provide the City Planning Division with a source for informed residents' perspectives on planning priorities and policies that impact the city as a whole" (City of Toronto, 2016).

The panel was independently chosen and is organised by MASS LBP, one of Canada's leading public deliberation organisations. Through the civic lottery process, 12,000 Torontonian households received an invitation from the city's chief planner, Jennifer Keesmaat, with a note from the mayor, John Tory, emphasising the importance of their potential contribution. The letter outlined the panel's purpose and remit, and asked candidates whether they were available on at least 14 of the 16 dates provided. In response, over 500 Torontonians applied to participate as panellists (503 volunteered and an additional 71 expressed interest in further information but were unable to participate due to conflicting schedules).

For the second stage of the civic lottery, a random group of 28 people was chosen among the respondents, controlling for age, gender, geography, household tenure, visible minority status (important for the city of Toronto, as 51% of the population are immigrants) and the guaranteed inclusion of at least one Aboriginal member. Daniel Fusca, the City of Toronto Planning Division's stakeholder engagement lead, praises the civic lottery process, saying: "It is a very effective way of getting a broad range of people involved. There is even one individual on the panel who was once homeless".

Anyone working for the City of Toronto or for a contractor for the City Planning Division, members of another official City of Toronto advisory body, and elected officials along with declared candidates seeking offices were not eligible to volunteer. As with all of MASS LBP's reference panels, the panellists are not paid, but are asked to donate their time as a form of public service. Any costs incurred, such as childcare or other caring responsibilities, food and travel are covered. The names of all of the panellists are published on the city's website, with a picture and a short autobiography, as well as a statement of their reasons for wanting to be on the panel.

During the first four training sessions, the 28 panellists heard 17 presentations from a variety of experts, stakeholders, policymakers and people working in the City Planning Division. The group established the guiding principles for planning in Toronto: inclusivity; safety and security; innovation; affordability and prosperity;

community wellbeing; and functionality. They also established their planning priorities for the panel: natural environment; housing; design; heritage; built form and the public realm; transportation; and the economy.

Each of the following meetings will tackle a variety of issues of strategic importance to the city and the City Planning Division, including transport projects, urban design guidelines, parks and recreation, and local area plans.

Speaking at the outset of the project, Fusca was optimistic about the panel and its ability to create a positive change for the city. He suggested that the panel was prompted by a study conducted within the planning division:

> We found that the people we were reaching through our typical engagements are English-speaking, male, well-educated homeowners over the age of 55. So we were looking for better ways of reaching youth, newcomers and renters. There was pressure on us to follow suit of the New York City planning boards [where 50 people are appointed to each Board by the borough president, with input from the city councillors], but the problem is that they work inconsistently, cost a lot, and yet are underfunded comparative to their required tasks. We also believe that the process of having councillors elect members risks leaving out large groups of people not already engaged in the political process. So we put out a request for a proposal for a more democratic process. MASS LBP's proposal for the Toronto Planning Review Panel came from there.

Costing a total of around $100,000 CAD (the equivalent of around £68,000 in October 2016), it is a modest sum for a panel of this size and scale. As all of the members are from the Toronto area, travel costs are low and translation is not required.

A few months in, the panel is still a work in progress. It is the first time that a panel of this nature is taking place: it is not about a single issue and members will meet over a longer period of time. Nonetheless, there have been some positive developments so far. Fusca is "amazed at the panellists: at their curiosity; their sophistication; their intelligence, and their desire to contribute something positive". When asked how the panel compares to typical forms of engagement, he responded:

> It is quite a difference. Public consultations are usually somewhat negative. People typically engage when they are motivated by self-interest, especially when they want to stop something from happening. It is refreshing to work with people focused on the positive and on providing constructive feedback.

The panel continues to do its work and a better evaluation can only come at its completion. However, press coverage thus far has been good and the city's leaders are supportive. Success, however, will depend on the outcomes. For Fusca:

> Success will be easy to identify, but hard to quantify. Largely, it will rest on four things. That the panellists feel their views were taken seriously. That the panellists learn and grow. If my colleagues see value, they will begin integrating the panel into planning process in a holistic way. And if we see people reporting on the panel's inputs in council reports.

Depending on these factors, the Planning Division can envisage a new panel of Torontonians being recruited for another panel after 2018. The idea is to institutionalise it, changing the relationship between the citizens of Toronto and City Hall.

AUSTRALIA

The Australian examples discussed in detail are outlined below. All of the other cases are listed and briefly described in the appendix.

Table 6.   Overview of long-form deliberative processes in Australia

Average	
Duration	Five full-day in-person meetings over three months
Number of participants	41
Number of invitations posted	8,400

The following examples were chosen for in-depth discussion as they have taken place at various levels of governance and are all on different topics, illustrating the breadth of possibilities that these processes can be used for, while at the same time highlighting the unifying characteristics between them.

Table 7.   Overview of in-depth Australian case studies

Level of governance	Topic	Duration	No. of invitations	No. of participants	Cost (AUD)
City	Melbourne People's Panel 2014	6 days	7,000	43	$144,650
State	Infrastructure Victoria 2016: 30-Year Plan	6 days	12,000	43 (x2)	$325,450
State	VicHealth 2015: We have a problem with obesity. How can we make it easier to eat better?	4 days	15,000	100	$221,750
State	Citizens' Jury on a Vibrant and Safe Nightlife for Adelaide 2013	5 days	24,000	43	$152,200
State	Citizens' Juries on the Nuclear Fuel Cycle 2016	4 days	25,000	50/350	$183,000

I. City of Melbourne People's Panel 2014

Melbourne is the largest city in Australia with significant population growth expected. In 2014, the council committed to a range of projects and long-term strategies that would require large-scale investment. The purpose of the People's Panel was to give recommendations to the City of Melbourne for its 10-year financial plan (worth $5bn AUD), helping determine how projects should be funded and which ones were priorities. The panel's remit was to reach agreement on how Melbourne can remain one of the most live-able cities in the world while maintaining a strong financial position in the future. The council agreed to listen to the panel's views and consider all recommendations when developing its financial plan. As part of this commitment, the council promised to meet with the panel and formally respond to all of its recommendations.

In late May 2014, the council and the newDemocracy Foundation (nDF), the independent organisation in charge of organising and running the panel, began the process with a planning meeting. This was to decide the background information and expert contributions to include, identify communication targets for submissions, decide on the dates and goals, agree the media strategy, and finalise venues.

Once this was all decided, 7,500 invitations from the lord mayor on behalf of the entire council were mailed to a random sample of citizens and students, with a three-week period to respond. Six thousand addresses were taken from the council's ratepayer database and 1,000 were made available from the University of Melbourne database. In the meantime, there was a call for public submissions and stakeholder briefings. Among the 2,000 people who responded, 45 panellists were randomly chosen, stratifying for age, gender, ratepayer status and location. As the nDF notes, this is not a "perfect" method, but ratepayer status is a good indicator of income and education, and it delivers a more representative sample than any other community process. Given that Melbourne is also a business hub, nDF also ensured that there was a mix of small and large businesses. There was also a mix of residents – both owner-occupiers and renters – in equal parts. Just as in judicial juries, participants were paid a per diem of $500 AUD to avoid exclusion due to financial hardship.

Once the panel was finalised, they received the welcome kit materials which had been decided upon in advance. Panellists were also invited to join a live online discussion group where they could speak with one another and propose expert speakers they would like to hear from during the meetings. At the end of August 2014, the panel met for the first time in person, starting the learning stage. They were welcomed by the lord mayor, introduced to the topic, and reminded about their influence and the wider context. As with all of nDF's citizens' juries, the panellists were also talked through the process, its precedents, and given an understanding about the inevitability of individual bias and the importance of constructive, critical thinking.

Among themselves, the group of 45 also agreed on the principles which would guide their participation and their decision-making: SMART (specific, measurable, achievable, realistic, timely); sustainable; forward-thinking; adds value to Melbourne; relevant to the remit and the challenges; and that recommendations should be 'considered' in terms of an awareness of their implications for people. After these principles were set, the panel heard from and questioned a number of experts who had been selected on the basis of the panel's prior online discussions. Panellists also identified speakers they wanted to hear from at future meetings.

Three weeks later, the panel met for a second time – the 'understanding' stage. Exploring the content from the background materials and hearing from more experts, the group continued learning about the various challenges the city is facing, proposed projects and other considerations, including costs and funding gaps. Once again, they ended the day by identifying what information they felt was still missing and other experts from whom they wanted to hear.

After a further three weeks, the panel turned to the 'focus' stage. After numerous weeks of reading, listening to experts, speaking with their friends and families, the panellists began thinking about what they might recommend to the council. Starting with a blank sheet of paper, they agreed on a structure and outline for their report and presentation.

Another three weeks later, they met again for the 'reflect, discuss, deliberate' stage. Returning to their structure, they discussed in small groups a long list of priorities and various funding models. Each group agreed on its top priorities, which were shared with the entire group so that collective priorities could be decided.

The final deliberation to determine their shared goals took place one week later. The session was focused on building consensus and fleshing out recommendations based on the priorities that had been identified. Panellists were also reminded about the decision-making principles they set out at the outset, with an emphasis on their desire to be SMART. In order for a recommendation to make it into the final report, an 80% supermajority was required in the group. In the end, the panel proposed 11 concrete recommendations to the council in an unedited report. It presented its recommendations to the lord mayor and councillors at a public meeting a few weeks later. Their proposals ranged from increased funding to address climate change (measures included vertical gardens, solar panels, waste management and recycling), to a five-year plan for introducing more bicycle lanes and physical barriers in the city, to decreasing expenditure on new capital works by 10% over 10 years and raising rates by inflation plus up to 2.5% per annum for 10 years.

The council considered the panel's proposals over the course of a few months, releasing their final 10-year financial plan seven months later. The final plan was, according to the city, "heavily influenced by [the] Council's People's Panel, a 43-member citizens' jury convened to advise on spending and revenue priorities for the next decade" (City of Melbourne, 2015). Accepting 10 out of 11 of the key recommendations, they also outlined their reasoning. In the city's final publication of the plan, all of the citizens' jury's recommendations are in their unedited form, with the council's response and an explanation alongside each of them.

A survey among the panel's members at the end of their final session found that 96% of the participants highly rated their involvement as a worthwhile experience (Molony, 2015). At the end of the deliberation process, the same survey indicated that participants had higher levels of confidence in the City of Melbourne, higher levels of internal and external efficacy (an individual's belief that they can understand politics or that political actors are responsive to them), and general satisfaction with the city's future direction.

In terms of the effectiveness of the consultation, an independent review of the public engagement process by Clear Horizon also found that it was good value for money in terms of effectiveness and economy. "The recommendations, i.e. the outcomes of the engagement process", it concluded, "are highly implementable" (Molony, 2015).

The Melbourne People's Panel was one of the most successful citizens' juries in Australia for a number of reasons: the problem was clear; the council was open to hearing the panel's proposals; and it accepted the vast majority of them, closing an $800-900m AUD budget hole.

2. Infrastructure Victoria 2016: 30-year Plan

At the end of 2015, Infrastructure Victoria (IV), an independent infrastructure body, was asked by the Victoria government to produce a 30-year plan. Instead of the typical public consultation procedure – drafting a plan and then sharing it for feedback – IV incorporated the consultation phase right from the start, commissioning the newDemocracy Foundation to organise and run two, independent randomly selected citizens' juries to co-design a draft plan. The remit was to determine how Victoria's infrastructure needs should be met, setting out which projects should be priorities and how they should be paid for. IV agreed that the unedited recommendations would be published and the chair of IV would respond to them directly in person. As the body's CEO, Michel Masson, explained: "We wanted this to be a strategy for the community and by the community and we are proud of achieving this aim through strong collaboration with the people of Victoria".

The two juries, each with around 43 people participating, took place in Melbourne, to capture urban views, and in Shepparton, to capture more rural perspectives. Both juries were asked to consider nine key infrastructure categories identified by IV, as well as any additional ones that they thought should be included. The juries formed one part of a three-tier, year-long engagement process. In addition to the juries, IV also engaged with the wider public through digital tools, the mass media, community groups and targeted stakeholder engagement. Stakeholders were invited to present their 'case' or 'evidence' to the juries, providing jurors with a key source of information. It meant that stakeholders were required to pass the scrutiny of a group of ordinary citizens, who are not experts, politicians or bureaucrats and are not part of any factions or susceptible to donors' wishes. IV's aim, by giving the community a genuine level of influence through a shared decision-making process, was to propose a plan built on public trust.

To choose the jury members, 14,000 people were randomly invited by post, drawn from Australia Post's databases to ensure a mix of tenants and owners, as well as those not on the electoral register, were reached. Letters were from the IV board to emphasise the importance of the task. Those invited could then register their interest in participating through an online portal. Jurors were chosen through a stratified random draw from this pool. Each participant was paid $500 AUD to participate in six full-day meetings over three months, with many hours spent reading information materials and public submissions in between. As with all of nDF's juries, the jurors' contact information was not provided to IV ahead of the first meeting, thus building public confidence that no 'vetting' could take place.

Both juries followed the same process of learning, understanding, focusing and deliberating on recommendations, meeting in person for a full Saturday every two to three weeks. At the start, jurors were briefed about how the process works, the wider context, the importance of their contribution, the inevitability of bias and the importance of critical thinking. In the early jury meetings, participants heard from a wide range of experts and stakeholders through a mix of panel presentations and 'speed dialogue' sessions, they read community submissions, requested more information and also heard from IV representatives.

Additionally, the jurors had an extensive range of online engagement opportunities in between the meetings. These included an 'expectations mapping' tool, which allowed people to see the gap between their own views and underlying factors such as current levels of expenditure, population growth estimates, subsidies versus user chargers by infrastructure type, and other relevant information. A 'VoteCompass' for infrastructure was also launched, allowing people to respond to a series of questions relating to people's values, which revealed preferences about infrastructure funding models.

Overall, the jurors were presented with three key sources of information which informed their deliberations. One was a 150-page information kit from IV, which explained in plain English the 'problem' and a number of possible solutions. This was objective in nature, with IV presenting its view in a clearly marked separate section. In addition, jurors received the unedited submissions from interest groups and stakeholders, which were placed in chronological order to help avoid bias. Finally, jurors were able to ask questions where they felt they needed more information at any point, with the answers made available to all participants.

Moving into the latter phases of the engagement process, the juries began focusing on priorities and funding options. A long list of ideas was narrowed down into 19 recommendations, with, once again, a consensus reached by requiring a supermajority of 80% of jurors to ensure a proposal's inclusion. Each report also included an appendix, however, which noted points of strong disagreement and a minority view.

The unedited report of both citizens' juries is available to view on the IV website, alongside a direct response from IV to each proposal that was made. Overall, it accepted 192 of the jurors' recommendations, disagreeing with just 13 of them. For each of those 13, IV provided a detailed explanation as to their position. In IV's final report on all of its consultation processes, released in October 2016, the reports of the citizens' juries are included in their unedited form as an appendix. In the body of the main report, those parts where the IV board was influenced or guided by a citizen's view are noted. IV's report has been presented to the Victoria government and was tabled in parliament on 8 December 2016.

3. VicHealth 2015: We have a problem with obesity. How can we make it easier to eat better?

VicHealth is an independent organisation which conducts research into health promotion and chronic disease prevention. It advises the Victoria government on findings which might be relevant to policymakers. As part of its work on obesity, VicHealth commissioned the newDemocracy Foundation in April 2015 to run an independent citizens' jury in response to the Obesity System Atlas's advice that effectively tackling obesity requires action from a broad range of multi-sector stakeholders.

The citizens' jury was larger than any of the others that nDF had organised until that point, consisting of 78 people from across the state. Twenty thousand people were randomly invited to participate through a mix of online and posted invitations, with addresses drawn from the 'VoteCompass' database, where at least 570,000 people had opted in to participate in events related to public policy, as well as two student databases to maximise the reach of 18–24 year olds. Of those who responded to the invitation, 117 people were randomly chosen, stratifying for age, gender and geography. The jury began with an online process, during which time a few people withdrew, either due to changes in personal circumstances or lack of time or interest. In the end, 78 people took part in the face-to-face meeting. The jurors were paid $250 AUD in total for their time, with accommodation and travelling costs also covered. The jury's remit was to provide concrete recommendations to a steering group for how to encourage people to eat better in Victoria. Its members agreed to respond to each request and indicate their ability to do what is proposed.

The steering group was made up of key decision-makers and influencers from government, the health sector, industry bodies, retailers, consumer advocates, local government, academia, NGOs, public health advocates and sporting bodies. It included: Australian Medical Association Victoria; Australian Beverages Council; Australian Food and Grocery Council; CHOICE (consumer advocacy group); City of Melbourne; Centre for Physical Activity and Nutrition Research at Deakin University; Coles (a supermarket chain); Foodbank Victoria; Obesity Policy Coalition; Tennis Australia; VicHealth; and the Department of Premier and Cabinet.

At the start, nDF worked with VicHealth and the steering group to identify the appropriate background materials and expert contributions to send to participants. They also contacted media partners and confirmed the final dates. As part of the jury's activities would take place online, nDF also selected the online platform services that would be used. Once this was completed, the 20,000 invites were sent out electronically and by post, with a four-week deadline for recruitment. When the jurors were selected, they were sent the information welcome kit by email, with a limited distribution via hard copy in the post.

In September 2015, an online introductory session for jurors was arranged to allow them to familiarise themselves with the material and recognise their initial attitudes, preconceptions and beliefs. The second online step was more intense, requiring around two hours of reading time, half an hour of posting and another half an hour of reading other jurors' contributions. The focus was on which documents or videos participants found the most interesting, what they learnt and what they wanted to share with the group. A second forum prompted reflection on the range of sources and whether they supported or conflicted with their own thoughts. The next online stage asked participants what further information they felt they needed to be better informed and which people and organisations they wanted to hear from in person. A few weeks later, a final online session moved the participants on to generating and refining their own ideas. Discussions were held about which ideas – however broad – they had been thinking about.

At the start of October, the jurors met in person for the learning phase. Welcomed by the premier and the steering group, the jurors' influence and the importance of their contribution were explained. The process, its precedents, an understanding of the inevitability of bias and the need for critical thinking were explained to the participants. The jurors started their discussions by agreeing the guidelines for participation, before beginning a 'speed dialogue' session with the experts who had been identified by the steering group and that the participants had said they wanted to hear from during their online discussions.

The second deliberation moved towards the deliberation phase. As the jurors had already spent around 7-8 hours engaging with information and with one another online, they began by discussing the ideas that had been proposed online. Exploring what would need to change and why from those ideas helped the group to move towards consensus and building a shared set of recommendations. The second half of the day was focused on incorporating the new information from the previous meeting into the recommendations. Reminded that their proposals had to be SMART (specific, measurable, actionable, realistic and with a time horizon), the jurors made revisions until these criteria were met. Overall, the jury made 20 recommendations. They ranged from introducing mandatory healthy eating and cooking as part of the school curriculum from pre-school to Year 10, to government-regulated health star labelling, making drinking fountains available and accessible in public places, introducing a 20% tax on high-added sugar drinks, and limiting the ability of food and beverage producers to market the healthy components of products which were actually unhealthy.

A few weeks later, after the steering group had had a chance to read through the jury's report, the participants reconvened for a final day to hear the responses. The group responded directly to each recommendation, identifying which aspects they were or were not able to enforce and why. The common response that is often used to dismiss policy proposals – that voters or citizens would not want such actions – was thus dispensed with. An insights report by VicHealth (2016) recognised that it was difficult for the steering group to respond collectively, as the stakeholders had different views on solutions depending on which interests they represented. Their replies were therefore set out individually based on what each organisation was prepared to communicate externally. However, a large majority

of the stakeholders (79%) saw the citizens' jury as an effective way
to involve Victoria's citizens in public decision-making. Half of the
stakeholders that VicHealth surveyed said that they would use the
jury's report directly in their work.

The effect of participation on the jurors is also worth exploring
when considering the 'success' of the process. VicHealth's survey
found that almost two-thirds of participants reported that if they
heard a citizens' jury process was commissioned by another government department, they would trust what it said; only three percent
said they would not do so. More than half (57%) of the jurors were
also moved to take personal action to address obesity as a result of
being involved, and nine in 10 jurors perceived VicHealth's role
and influence in relation to action on obesity as very or somewhat
effective.

At the time of writing, it has only been a few months since the
jury's recommendations to government, industry and public health
advocates were presented. VicHealth is currently monitoring their
actions and working actively with policymakers, public health and
consumer advocates and industry to promote the jury's proposals.

4. Citizens' Jury on a Vibrant and Safe Nightlife for Adelaide 2013

How do you balance community safety and personal freedom to
achieve a vibrant and safe nightlife? It is a question that many city
leaders contemplate, with repercussions for commerce, infrastructure, alcohol licensing, transport, health, education and entertain-
ment. In 2013, the Premier and Cabinet's office in South Australia
took a new approach to finding an answer in Adelaide. It brought
together 43 randomly selected people from Greater Adelaide to form
a citizens' jury, which was organised and run by the newDemocracy
Foundation, to advise government on reform options.

The jurors were selected with a rigorous two-stage recruitment approach. Twenty-four thousand citizens from across greater
Adelaide were randomly invited by the premier, Jay Weatherill,

to participate. The addresses were drawn from a mixture of the Australian Post database as well as university and TAFE (Australia's largest vocational education and training provider) databases to help maximise the response rate of 18-24 year olds. Those who responded to the invitation were then stratified by age, gender and geography to ensure a more representative group of participants. They were each paid $400 AUD for participating so as not to deter those facing financial hardship from considering the invitation.

Before the jury's first meeting, nDF worked with the premier's engagement team to identify the information that would need to be included in the welcome kits and the key speakers and stakeholders to invite for the 'learning' phases of the deliberative process. The media was also extensively briefed, ensuring that the public could hold the government to account to respond to the jury's recommendations.

During six full-day meetings over the course of more than three months, the jurors read a wide array of information, heard from a broad range of experts, stakeholders, businesses, health specialists, and others, read submissions from their fellow citizens, deliberated with one another, and came to a consensus about their shared goals. They produced seven key recommendations, presenting them directly to the premier at the end of October 2013. The jury's proposals included:

- "The creation of one central source of event and activity information. Adelaide has a lot of events and activities to offer, but the information regarding them is scattered.
- Encourage a diversity of businesses to trade in the night-time economy to augment the current licensed business sector.
- Review the SA Liquor Licensing Act (1997) to ensure that licenses are granted and enforced to enhance vibrancy, continuity and equity in Adelaide.
- The State Government needs to remove vibrancy barriers to encourage people to enter Adelaide's CBD using an integrated transport system that recognises all modes of transport.

- The jury values, and encourages the government to preserve, the use of education programs in school and community groups to promote safety.
- Establish an independent advisory body to oversee the strategic planning of infrastructure projects with consideration for safety and vibrancy.
- Establish an 'Injury and Outcome Reporting System'" (Citizens' Jury on a Vibrant and Safe Nightlife in Adelaide, 2013).

These are, of course, summaries; the jury expanded upon and justified each of these points in a 15-page report for the premier, with more detailed sub-recommendations in each category. Their recommendations were considered in their unedited form by the cabinet and parliament. Ultimately, all of them were accepted. The South Australian government published a series of status updates about the new initiatives that arose from the jury's recommendations, publishing public reports on the YourSAy website in August 2014, January 2015 and September 2015. The latest update shows that the government has made significant strides in meeting all of the jury's proposals, and has done so in a clear, easy-to-access way.

Beyond making a direct impact on policy, the citizens' jury also influenced a change in both the government's and the wider public's views about citizen engagement in policymaking. "It was successful in changing people's perceptions that things could be done differently", according to Gail Fairlamb, strategic engagement director in the Department of the Premier and Cabinet. The result of the jury prompted the government's report on democratic innovation, Reforming Democracy: Deciding, Designing and Delivering Together (2015). It explored the use of deliberative democracy projects as well as digital tools, crowd sourcing, collaborative working and design thinking approaches to various aspects of government activity. The premier's office has since commissioned three more citizens' juries – one on cyclists and motorists sharing the roads safely, one on dog and cat laws (related to euthanasia, puppy farm cruelty, etc.) and most recently on the nuclear fuel cycle, which is detailed as the last case study in this book. Moreover, Fairlamb explains that "the increased use of citizens' juries and other forms of public engagement [by the South Australian government] means that public awareness is growing". It seems that the government has begun institutionalising the involvement of citizens in public decision-making, driven by the philosophy of 'better together'.

5. Citizens' Juries on the Nuclear Fuel Cycle 2016

The final case study in this book came to an end shortly before publication, so its effectiveness cannot be evaluated in the same way as the other examples. It is worth highlighting, however, due to its unique topic and structure as a complement to a royal commission process. The South Australian government was facing a difficult decision about whether or not to continue to pursue opportunities related to the nuclear fuel cycle, including mining and milling, enrichment and fuel fabrication, and electricity generation as well as fuel waste management and storage.

Given the particularly complex nature of the problem, a royal commission was established to inform the government's decision-making. However, the premier was aware that this alone would not be sufficient in order to engage the wider public and gain citizens' support for whatever decision was eventually taken. Most people do not read royal commission reports and most people believe that public consultations are often 'tick-box' exercises where a decision has already been taken or is firmly in mind.

To get around this dual dilemma, the South Australian government asked the newDemocracy Foundation to run and organise two citizens' juries to complement the royal commission. One of these juries, with 54 randomly selected people, would first set the agenda, determining the most important aspects of the commission's findings that everyone in South Australia should consider. Its task was to create an accessible way for other citizens in the state to explore the 318-page commission report. It would not be subject to any partisan or interest-group perspectives, a criticism to which a government, business sector or environmental group might be prone. This jury differed in a crucial way to all the others discussed in this book: rather than giving recommendations to a minister, a premier, a mayor or other public authority, its report was directed at the entire population of South Australia: 1,039,000 fellow citizens. The rationale, however, was the same: to build trust.

A second, larger citizens' jury with 350 randomly selected South Australians – including the 54 individuals from the first jury – will review all of the feedback from the wider community engagement. Its remit is to recommend to the government whether the state should continue to pursue opportunities related to the nuclear fuel cycle. Only the first weekend of meetings at the beginning of October 2016 had taken place at the time of writing.

Twenty-five thousand invitations were sent to randomly chosen addresses from the Australia Post database to recruit the jury members. Of those who replied, a stratified random sample of 54 was chosen for the first jury, controlling for age, gender and location according to census data. The jury had 16 renters and 34 homeowners and was gender-balanced. Forty-two people lived in the capital, Adelaide, and 12 lived in regional South Australia. There was a balanced mix of people from all age groups.

As its remit was to produce a summary making sense of the royal commission report, the first jury was intensely focused on learning. The participants were presented with many of the sources upon which the commission had relied in writing its report. At the end of their first full weekend of hearing from various people within the royal commission and a group of those who had made a submission to the commission, the jurors then requested additional information from any source they wanted to hear from. During their second weekend together, the jurors heard from the additional experts they had requested and drafted their summary document to help South Australians assess the royal commission report. The jury's report included a set of principles which they felt people should consider when discussing the state's involvement in the nuclear fuel cycle, as well as key points on the topics covered in the royal commission's report:

safety; the need to gather informed community consent; and the economic risks and benefits. It also highlighted specific aspects of the report itself which were worth reading (Nuclear Fuel Cycle Citizens' Jury, 2016). The jury's unedited text was transformed into a visual, easy-to-access document available through the South Australian government and gained media attention. It was disseminated over the course of a few months before the second jury took place.

Over the course of three weekends in October and November 2016, 350 South Australians heard from a wide range of experts, reviewed the first jury's summary of the royal commission's report and deliberated with one another to find common ground on the following, specific question: "Under what circumstances, if any, could South Australia pursue the opportunity to store and dispose of nuclear waste from other countries?"

The jury's agenda, witness list, news, discussion guide, and background information about all of the participants is available on the YourSAy website. Anybody could also register their interest in being an observer – among those who indicated they wanted to do this online, 20 were selected to be taken on a tour of the second jury's proceedings, to build wider trust in the process. The jury's deliberations were also live-streamed and videoed for anyone from the public to watch.

The jury's verdict at the end of the process was a resounding 'no' to the question. At the time of writing, an official response from Weatherill is awaited. Framing it may be tricky: the jury's outcome contradicts the royal commission's recommendations and arguably goes against what many experts and stakeholders would like to see happen. One to watch for interested observers.

SHORTCOMINGS OF LONG-FORM DELIBERATIVE PROCESSES

Despite their usefulness and effectiveness, it is worth discussing some of the shortcomings or tensions that arise with long-form deliberations, namely the potential of politicisation, the varied role of the media, the evolving use of long-form deliberation techniques on big issues and the difficult question of defining 'success'.

First, by their nature, long-form deliberations are most often commissioned by governments (although they are also sometimes commissioned by chief executives or directors of other public authorities, such as hospitals). This means that they are also seen as being commissioned by a single political party, thus subject to politicisation. According to Matt Ryan, director of public policy and strategy at the Australian Centre for Social Innovation and former deputy chief of staff to Jay Weatherill:

> The actors in the current decision-making system almost always react with cynicism to the process. Perhaps unsurprisingly so. For political parties not forming government, parliament is their main form of engagement in public debate. Anything that diminishes their role in urging the consideration of alternative points of view, a role which citizens in a deliberative process often undertake and even reconcile, is threatening to their influence and profile. In effect, it reduces their ability to garner the 'political capital' required to win government. This seems to be a product of the adversarial quality of the Westminster system which pits a government against an opposition.

This is an important consideration and raises the question of whether long-form deliberations are also a tool that should be used more often by parliamentary select committees, given their multiparty membership and thus non-partisan aims. Committee members still have the necessary authority of being elected representatives, with the opportunity of feeding in the findings of deliberative processes into legislative scrutiny and parliamentary debate. But their non-party political goals alter the dynamics and would thus make the process less subject to cynical politicking.

Second, the role of the media is another important question. While the media brings publicity which is imperative to the process, those on the commissioning side have also had varied experiences with the media in relation to democratic reforms. In spite – or perhaps because – of criticisms about the state of politics and the lack of trust in politicians, there is sometimes criticism of attempts to remedy it. In some ways, the long-form deliberative process is seen as undermining the watchdog role of the media, with citizens acting on behalf of other citizens to play a 'gatekeeping' role. Furthermore, the collaboration and consensus-seeking which is at the heart of long-form deliberations is not particularly news-worthy, as the point is precisely to give people the time and space to reflect on and discuss at length a controversial issue in a non-adversarial way; the opposite of contentious sound-bites which the media feeds upon. Gaining the right balance in coverage to raise awareness and critique of the process is delicate.

Third, as has hopefully been clear throughout this book, long-form deliberative practices are not the solution for solving every type of public problem. They work best for policy issues where no single solution is clear, multiple trade-offs and priorities must be weighed, and more than one possible path forward is viable. Arguably, they are also better used when an issue is salient, but not yet at the point of controversy, where strong opposition has not already been mobilised and ingrained. As the long-form deliberative process has been experimented with more and more, it has also been applied to issues of greater and greater importance.

The skills required to ensure the process is carried out rigorously and methodically thus become even more significant. As Ryan argues, "not only does more attention need to be paid to interfaces with parliament and the media, but also the broader population and large stakeholder interests. Stakeholder management and communications become ever more important to ensure trust in the process". This was a sentiment that came up numerous times during interviews with various people in positions of power in both Canada and Australia.

One response has been to increase the size of the jury, which has been more common in Australia than in Canada. However, the difficulty of managing larger juries, the trade-off between high-quality deliberation and greater 'representativeness' must also be taken into account. Beyond 50 people, the balance arguably begins to tip away from quality. Is the best way of enlarging a deliberative process merely to increase the numbers, as one would do with an opinion poll? It is questionable whether this is congruent with the aims and objectives of the process in the first place.

Finally, it is recognised that there are different definitions of 'success' when it comes to the outcome of a long-form deliberation. These may relate to the impact on policy, the broader shaping of public debate, the strengthening of participants' agency and the encouragement of internal organisational change with regard to how decisions are made. The overarching objective can also be seen as increasing social capital in whatever form that takes. Not all of these aspects can be concretely measured, and often need time for the impact to be witnessed. More research is also required on the longer-term impact of participating in a deliberative process, in particular how it affects participants' later political and civic engagement.

PUBLIC CONSULTATION AND ENGAGEMENT IN THE UK

ROYAL COMMISSIONS, INQUIRIES AND TRADITIONAL CONSULTATIONS

After examining the case studies of best practice in Canada and Australia, it is worth reflecting on how difficult and contentious policy decisions are often currently resolved in the United Kingdom. Often, they tend to take the form of either royal commissions, inquiries or more traditional public consultations – town hall meetings, online surveys, focus groups, short deliberative events or open calls for public responses. While each of these forms of public consultation has its merits, and is appropriate dependent on the nature of the problem, they also have their downsides. Comparing them to the use of long-form deliberative processes in Canada and Australia highlights how similar dilemmas can be solved in different ways, which may be more effective, legitimate or cost-efficient.

As briefly mentioned in the introduction, royal commissions and independent inquiries have often been the chosen route for absolving representative politics of its representative responsibility. Royal commissions are ad hoc advisory committees, appointed by the government (in the name of the Crown) for a specific advisory or investigatory purpose. The average royal commission takes two to four years to report (Riddell and Barlow, 2013). They have examined, among other topics, the future of the constitution, capital punishment, the press, police, gambling and local government. Overall, however, as Riddell and Barlow convincingly argue, the track record of royal commissions is poor – they take a long time and often become irrelevant thus leaving their recommendations ignored.

More recently, the model of the royal commission has been slimmed down to more rapidly reporting inquiries. At least in theory; inquiries are meant to last no more than 18 months. In reality, they have often lasted longer than commissions, leading to the same issue of their recommendations becoming irrelevant by the time of reporting. Even when their proposals are highly salient – as with the Davies inquiry on London airport capacity, for instance – it does not mean that action will follow. Although inquiries are supposed to have concrete terms of reference, transparent procedures, thoughtful leadership and strict time restrictions, these characteristics do not prevent them from being used as a political delaying tactic for making hard choices, where, no matter which decision is taken, somebody will be upset. Although this can be said of any consultation procedure, it is arguable that some approaches are more likely to win public support and legitimacy than others.

Besides their easily ignored time restrictions, public inquiries also cost the public a great deal of money. While this varies – the Turner review on pensions cost taxpayers £1.6m, while the Davies inquiry cost around £20m—it is safe to say that the inquiry process is one of the costliest options for public bodies wanting independent recommendations to help them gain legitimacy for their actions. Furthermore, the independence of inquiries is also questionable, as their membership is often composed of, and dominated by, former ministers and civil service permanent secretaries, who bring with them plentiful prior baggage.

On the other hand, the UK government, devolved governments and other public bodies hold thousands of public consultations every year. Some estimates have suggested that each local authority spends more than £2m annually, with over £1bn spent by the UK public sector as a whole (Involve, 2005). The vast majority of these take place in the form of online consultations accessible through the UK government website, where people are asked to fill in a response form by a certain deadline. While it was not possible to find exact numbers and demographics of respondents to these consultations, it is reasonable to assume that most Britons do not regularly check their government's website to see which consultations they are currently being asked to respond to. Rather, responses tend to come from a self-selecting demographic with a special interest involved. Other forms of consultation by public bodies, regulators and government departments commonly include online or telephone surveys, focus groups or deliberative events. These can be more representative of the wider public, but are usually limited to gathering the public's instinctive opinions when they have not had the time or the resources to contemplate all aspects of the topic at hand.

The reliance of government and public bodies on commissions, inquiries and traditional consultation methods in the UK is arguably one of the reasons why the solutions to contentious policy dilemmas have been frequently delayed. Infrastructure investment choices, such as airport expansion, a new high-speed rail project and the future of the Hinkley Point nuclear power station, are just a few of the major decisions that have suffered postponements amid public outcry in recent years. Without strong public support for them, a raft of proposals from the government's child obesity strategy were cut after Theresa May became prime minister. In the meantime, the cost of inaction for political reasons has been large, as the numerous inquiries and consultations on these topics have run into the millions of pounds. When it comes to tough policy choices, where public backing is important for gaining the legitimacy to act, British public bodies could learn a valuable lesson from the Canadians and Australians: there are many benefits to adding a considered citizens' view to public decision-making.

BEEN THERE, DONE THAT? PAST EXPERIMENTS WITH CITIZENS' JURIES IN THE UK

Some will argue that the use of citizens' juries in policymaking is nothing new in British politics. The New Labour governments under Tony Blair and Gordon Brown promoted them as a "big idea" and an "innovation in democracy" (Maer, 2007). Over 100 citizens' juries were held on a wide range of issues – from health care to education and decency on television (Delap, 2001). In some ways, they were similar to long-form deliberative processes in that they were commissioned by someone in authority (government) with the remit of providing advice on a matter of policy. Participants were randomly selected and given the time to deliberate on their ideas and seek information to help them reach decisions. But their size, scope, duration and methodology differed significantly to the case studies from Canada and Australia discussed in the previous section (see Table 1).

Table 8. Key differences between UK citizens' juries and long-form deliberative processes

	Citizens' juries (UK)	Long-form deliberative processes (Canada and Australia)
Size	12 to 24 people	28 to 48 people
Duration	Up to 4.5 days	2 to 3 months
Number of face-to-face meetings	1 to 4.5 days	4 to 6 days
Recruitment method	Varied, often with the use of recruiters	Transparent two-stage random selection process: (1) Random invitations to participate sent to 10,000-20,000 people; (2) Among those who respond, a random-stratified sample is chosen based on age, gender and either geography or housing tenure
Remit	Policy scrutiny: Often to provide advice or recommendations about a proposed policy	Policy formation and development: To start with a blank page, consider all the information and develop recommendations

While their use was widespread over a short period of time, the reactions and effectiveness were mixed. Some have argued that the citizens' juries successfully built trust and established new communities but were also expensive and time-consuming mechanisms (Delap, 2001). Overall, the participants were found to be willing and enthusiastic, encouraged that their voice would be taken seriously. However, the commitment from the policymakers initiating the juries was not always evident or publicly affirmed, leaving them open to suspicion about decisions having already been taken ahead of time; the citizens' juries were seen as a device for political legitimisation. Given that jurors were often only convened to meet for one day (and never more than four and a half days), this concern was justified. How is it possible for a group of randomly selected people to grasp a complex problem about which they may have had little or no prior knowledge, hear from all the relevant experts and stakeholders, deliberate with one another, consider trade-offs, determine priorities, and develop concrete recommendations within so little time? The notion that this must somehow be a 'fix' is a natural response in this scenario. It is one of the reasons why MASS LBP in Canada always asks the public authorities with which it works to sign a dual contract, promising to publicly address the recommendations of the citizens' panels.

In addition, the juries conducted in the latter part of the 2000s were also exorbitantly costly, especially when compared with the modest costs associated with the much more rigorous long-form deliberative processes detailed in the previous section. For example, one citizens' jury which held five meetings for the Department for Children, Schools and Families cost £467,704. Another citizens' jury (which was, in fact, nine separate one-day deliberative events) in September 2007 cost £868,930 (Maer, 2007). The cost breakdowns are not detailed further.

With the financial crisis in 2008, the government understandably had bigger problems to deal with than cultivating better public engagement, and the use of citizens' juries slowed. But the question as to why the use of citizens' juries has not caught on remains pertinent and is important for understanding whether long-form deliberative processes could be a useful policymaking device in the UK.

A number of possible explanations exist. Innovation is most likely to be attempted when the risk is not seen as too great, and the outcome is viewed as potentially significant. The high costs associated with citizens' juries mean that the risk was perhaps perceived as too large. But this is more a design flaw of the processes that took place rather than an inherent flaw in the principle of deliberative processes more generally. The examples in this study highlight that people often end up making decisions that are not a million miles away from existing policies or ideas proposed by experts. They are sometimes slightly more radical, but remain practical and deliverable. Quite often, particularly on social issues, citizens find that the problem is not with government so much as it is with the public at large, which itself needs to change. Why go through the bother of the process in this case? Because, with declining levels of trust in elected officials and in government, the decision-making process is as important as the decisions themselves. When people have a chance to have a genuine say in making the decisions affecting their lives, the policies that result are perceived as more legitimate and public support for them increases.

Furthermore, it is possible to mitigate the risks. If established properly, the risk of a bad outcome is low. Politicians do not need to promise to abide by the recommendations, simply to engage with them seriously, explaining why they can or cannot adopt certain ideas. Since the late 1990s and early 2000s, the world has gone digital. Conducting a transparent process, with wide public reach via the media and access to a large array of experts, has never been easier. With technology, the entire process can also become completely transparent. Everyone can see which experts informed the citizens' jury and how the process was conducted. Transparency and an understanding of the fairness involved in the process can also help foster legitimacy and trust. Moreover, the Canadian and Australian examples of long-form deliberations also demonstrate that success comes from asking citizens to work on tangible and distinct issues, rather than expansive or aspirational questions which might intrude into high politics.

There is also a question of whether institutional inertia and cultural factors played a role. Is there simply an aversion to change and an acceptance of paternalism in the UK? Maybe, but this line of reasoning is weaker in the wake of the referendum on EU membership, where Britons resoundingly opted for groundbreaking institutional change.

The most convincing explanation is that citizens' juries and other forms of deliberative democracy have caught on in countries that are more federal in character than the UK and where significant powers are devolved to regional and municipal levels. Of the case studies from Canada and Australia, the majority are from the city and state or provincial level, where governments nonetheless have significant authority. While the UK remains more centralised than both of its Commonwealth partners, devolution is on the political agenda, with numerous cities and city regions gaining new mayors and powers in the coming years. It could be a great opportunity for the UK to draw inspiration from overseas and renew its democratic institutions.

Another key reason why long-form deliberations have proliferated in both Canada and Australia over the past few years is the common factor of having independent companies and organisations that have professionalised the discipline, particularly MASS LBP in Canada and the newDemocracy Foundation in Australia. By doing so, they have ensured cost-efficiency and standardisation, instigating a rigorous methodology, based on deliberative theory and evidence of what works, and thereby refining and institutionalising the process.

Finally, a key factor is the fiscal situation. The UK will continue to operate tight budgets for the next decade, meaning choices about public spending and public services become ever harder. However, this makes the need for engaging citizens directly in shaping the policies that affect them, renewing Britain's democracy and strengthening the effectiveness and legitimacy of policies that will endure long-term scrutiny more important than ever.

RECENT EXPERIMENTS WITH CITIZENS' JURIES OR CITIZENS' ASSEMBLIES IN THE UK

The citizens' juries which were established under New Labour are not the sum total of the UK's experimentation with deliberative democracy. More recently, a number of mostly academic examples of democratic innovation have also been taking place. Two examples are notable. The first case is the citizens' juries on wind farm development in Scotland, run by researchers from the University of Edinburgh and the University of Strathclyde. The second case is two citizens' assemblies on devolution in Southampton and Sheffield run by the Crick Centre at the University of Sheffield and the Electoral Reform Society. While they again differ from long-form deliberative processes in many respects – in particular, in duration and remit – they nonetheless offer some interesting insights.

Citizens' Juries on Wind Farm Development in Scotland

The citizens' juries on onshore wind farm development in Scotland took place over two Saturdays in October 2013 and February 2014. Three groups of 15-20 people spent time developing and agreeing on a list of principles, listening to speakers, and discussing the following question: "There are strong views on wind farms in Scotland, with some people being strongly opposed, others being strongly in favour and a range of opinions in between. What should be the key principles for deciding about wind farm development, and why?"

The three jury locations were similar in size and rural characteristics, but differed in their exposure to wind farm developments: one was close to an existing wind farm (Aberfeldy), one had a wind farm proposal in the vicinity (Helensburgh) and a third had no existing or proposed wind farms (Coldstream). In terms of length of time and size of groups, the juries were similar to those which had occurred under New Labour.

However, unlike those juries, these were not commissioned by government, but were led by researchers from the University of

Edinburgh and the University of Strathclyde, in collaboration with colleagues at the University of the West of Scotland, Queen Margaret University, Robert Gordon University and Glasgow University. In addition to the universities, the organisers included What Works Scotland, ClimateXChange and the Edinburgh Centre for Carbon Innovation, and was overseen by a stewarding board with six members. The aim, therefore, was not to directly advise on government policy, but for the researchers to understand how deliberative processes can be used to engage citizens on complex public issues and learn about citizens' views on wind farms before and after the deliberative process.

Each of the three juries developed in the same way:

- 'Information phase' (day 1: an introduction to the process and learning from experts and advocates);
- 'Reflection phase' (two to three weeks in between the day-long events for jurors to take away information and receive responses to unanswered questions);
- And the 'deliberation phase' (day 2: jurors set the agenda and worked together to agree a set of principles to guide decisions about wind farm development).

The key findings were that citizens from different backgrounds are able to address complex policy problems when they have adequate time and information to do so as part of a fair and engaging process. The jurors engaged with one another's perspectives and changed their minds over time. Common themes emerged across the three juries, reflecting common values and tensions on the topic. Overall, the individuals that took part in the juries found the process enjoyable and rewarding, building their civic abilities.

The researchers also took away some key lessons for deliberative engagement related to: recruitment; time; design and facilitation; improvisation; and social space. Gathering a diverse group of people was one of the more challenging aspects of their project given the small group size. Most of the shortcomings were attributed to the limited amount of time, with the researchers saying that at least a third day of deliberation in person would have made a considerable difference to the process and outcomes. For a citizens' jury to be successful, experienced facilitators are imperative to create an environment in which different styles of learning, dialogue and deliberation can take place. Furthermore, regardless of the degree of preparation done ahead of time, there will always be a need to improvise and the organising team must be ready to be responsive and positive. Finally, a collaborative environment, where disagreement can be openly explored, requires establishing a social space between the participants through breaks, where 'relational capital' can be created.

Furthermore, it is worth noting that one of the outcomes of the project was to provide evidence to the Scottish government about the value of mini-publics. Scotland's new National Standards for Community Engagement, launched in September 2016, reference mini-publics and have been re-developed to aid in the implementation of the Community Empowerment (Scotland) Act 2015. This legislation incorporates new duties and provisions for public authorities to place deliberative engagement processes at the heart of their work.

Citizens' Assemblies on Devolution in Southampton and Sheffield

A second worthwhile experiment took place in 2015. In the lead-up to the 2015 general election, Democracy Matters was formed. This was a group led by Matthew Flinders at the Crick Centre in partnership with the Electoral Reform Society and academics from the universities of Westminster and Southampton and University College London. The premise was that a number of political parties were promising to support a constitutional convention to involve the public in discussions about the future shape of the union and the devolution deals that were beginning to take shape. Democracy Matters applied for an emergency grant from the ESRC to run two citizens' assemblies on devolution, which could have been expanded in the event of a constitutional convention. The group reacted quickly after the election when the Conservatives – the only party not to support a convention – won a majority, shifting the focus away from a UK-wide set-up towards one that looked directly at the new government's plans for devolution within England. Two areas in which deals were at different stages of negotiation were thus chosen. Assembly North took place in Sheffield and Assembly South in Southampton.

As in the case of the wind farm citizens' juries, it is worth keeping in mind that the assemblies were conducted partly for academic, rather than government decision-making, purposes. However, the aim of the organisers was also that the assemblies could be integrated into, as well as help shape, the government's future plans. The researchers sought to test a number of hypotheses:

- Does the inclusion of politicians in the deliberations alter their dynamics?
- Can ordinary members of the public, when given time and support, engage effectively in complex policy choices?
- Are citizens' assemblies better at debating issues than traditional assemblies, given they are not riven by partisan divides?
- Does deliberation promote reasoned opinion change?
- Does participation in a deliberative process enhance members' attitudes towards engagement with politics?
- Does participation affect members' feeling of efficacy, their sense of their ability to participate effectively in politics?

The two assemblies differed from one another in one key respect: Assembly North was composed entirely of 45 citizens, whereas Assembly South was made up of 30 citizens and 15 politicians. In reality, these numbers were smaller due to no-shows: the northern assembly had 32 participants and its southern counterpart had 23 citizens and six politicians take part. Of those who did participate, almost all of them came to both weekends – there were four dropouts in total, all due to illness. The two assemblies each met for two full weekends in October and November 2015 on staggered weekends.

There were four distinct phases to the citizens' assemblies:

- 'Learning phase' (briefing materials available before the first weekend which summarised current local government arrangements, outlined a variety of reform options and provided other background information; the first weekend was largely devoted to learning about reform options);
- 'Consultation phase' (began the first weekend and continued the second weekend; an opportunity to hear from local councillors, experts from universities and thinktanks, and campaigners);
- 'Deliberation phase' (although partly built into the entirety of the two weekends, the last part of the second weekend was structured with small-group discussions to allow members to begin working towards their own considered solutions);
- 'Shared decisions phase' (much shorter than the others and mainly consisted of voting on certain proposals).

The Democracy Matters group recognised both the positive elements and the lessons to be kept in mind for future deliberative democratic endeavours. As with the wind farm citizens' juries, the researchers found that with time and support, citizens are more than capable of engaging with difficult questions about complex issues and coming to evidence-based conclusions. Moreover, they found that participants were not 'anti-politician' or 'anti-politics,' but had a strong desire to do politics differently. A post-assembly survey found that participants enjoyed themselves and learnt a great deal through the process.

On the other hand, the researchers reflected that "recruitment, resources and realism" were three main areas where lessons were learnt. Due to the recruitment process with YouGov relying on their panels, there was an extremely high no-show rate, resulting in rather unrepresentative groups at both assemblies. The Democracy Matters group also reflected that what appeared to be a generous budget

(£200,000) was quickly eaten up by hotels, food and refreshments, training facilitators, website creation and maintenance, preparing information materials, booking transport, bringing international advisers to the UK, organising childcare, hiring trained facilitators, and paying staff members. In addition to this budget, the assemblies were possible due to contributions in kind, such as time dedicated by academic leads, volunteers helping run the events and speakers not being paid except for their travel expenses. Of course, other demo-cratic institutions, whether at Westminster, the devolved parliaments or local authorities, all cost money to be run. Seen in this context, the researchers argue that the costs of deliberative democracy are worthwhile.

Finally, the election of a majority Conservative government in 2015 took a bit of wind out of the project's sails, as there was less interest from politicians in a constitutional convention. This high-lights the importance of having authority figures supportive of the process for there to be a long-term impact on policy and for citizens to be willing to participate in such a time-intensive process. In short, the process needs to be meaningful and be seen to be so.

LESSONS LEARNT

There are four main lessons from the Scottish and English academic experiments:

- Meaningful political backing and engagement is necessary;
- The recruitment process must be transparent and rigorous;
- Adequate time is required;
- And the presence of an organisation which is experienced in organ-ising and running long-form deliberative processes helps to keep costs down and to maintain a rigorous, standardised methodology.

When compared to the long-form deliberative processes which have taken place in Canada and Australia, none of these four elements – all of which have an impact on the outcome – was entirely evident in the recent British trials.

Meaningful political backing and engagement and recruitment go hand in hand. The ability to recruit a broad cross-section of people partly stems from someone in government – who is in a position to act on the group's recommendations – commissioning the process. Without this, it is more difficult to interest people who are not impassioned activists to give up their time to learn about and discuss a complex policy issue. What kind of individual is willing to give up their free weekends to submerge themselves in the intricacies of planning policy, for instance, when there is nobody in a position of power to listen to the outcome of their deliberations? The likelihood is that those who are willing to participate in this instance are much more likely than the average person to be interested in politics or to be highly engaged with the issue at hand, which was indeed the case with the citizens' assemblies on devolution (Flinders *et al.,* 2016).

Furthermore, the recruitment design equally has an impact on the outcome. In the British scenarios, using a recruiter who is selecting participants from a panel means that, from the outset, it is not a truly random selection, as the only people who have a chance of being invited to participate are those who have signed up to a pollster's panel. The reason that pollsters need to adjust their weightings is because these panels are often not representative of the wider public. On the other hand, the two-stage lottery process used in both Canada and Australia means that everybody has an equal chance of receiving an invitation to participate in the first place. A disproportionate number of people from certain demographics tend to respond to this, but the stratification by age, gender and geography or housing tenure ensures that a balance is achieved in the final group. It is not a perfect method either, but it is the best way of bringing a wide-ranging cross-section of people together. This matters because greater diversity within a group leads to better deliberation, as a wider array of perspectives is considered (Kao and Couzin, 2014).

Arguably, the recruitment process also has an impact on participation and retention rates. It is notable that in the Canadian and Australian cases of long-form deliberative processes, where individuals are asked to give up more of their time than in either of the British cases, there have almost never been any drop-outs. This is not the result of monetary reward: in Canada participants simply have their expenses covered, while in Australia they are given only a small honorarium. Rather, it makes a difference for participants to be invited with an official government letter that comes directly from their premier, minister, mayor or other government official, asking them to represent their community and promising to listen to their recommendations and ideas at the end.

The length of time which participants met for was also arguably not sufficient. While a few days spread over a short period of time can show that citizens are thoughtful and capable of understanding complexity, willing to change their minds, and take this type of task seriously, it is perhaps not long enough for people to become reasonably informed about a multifaceted topic and come to a consensus about concrete and actionable proposals.

Finally, the Canadian and Australian examples highlight the value of having independent organisations dedicated to organising and running long-form deliberative processes (alongside other citizen engagement and consultations). They have established a standardised process and rigorous methodology, underpinned by theoretical research as well as evidence of what works. Having this in place, alongside the logistical structures of the recruitment process and a team familiar with all aspects of long-form deliberations, helps to reduce both time and the costs of running such initiatives.

Despite these shortcomings, the academic research on this topic is valuable, as it underlines that people are willing and able to contribute to solving public policy dilemmas, and that government would benefit from seeing the public as a resource to be tapped rather than a risk to be managed.

CONCLUSION

One of the key questions contemplated in the introduction of this book was: how should we solve complex and difficult problems in a democratic society? One of the potential answers is that long-form deliberative processes, where randomly selected citizens meet many times over numerous months to give recommendations about pressing public problems, should be part of the solution. Developing these new inclusive institutions can encourage constructive public debate that helps us reconcile conflicting values and aspirations.

Long-form deliberative processes are clearly not the answer to every type of public policy dilemma. But they are a good way for public bodies to gain a considered view from citizens. It allows a public institution to say: "The issue is obviously tough, but we put it to the people, they had access to all the information, they discussed the questions, they listened to each other to find common ground, and this is what they wanted". But these processes are about more than gaining legitimacy. As the 50 examples in this book alone highlight, when given the time and the resources, people come up with sensible ideas, meaning that political institutions also garner concrete, achievable, pragmatic and costed recommendations. The costs from the highlighted case studies also show that this need not be exorbitantly expensive; rather, it is perfectly feasible within the type of budget that most public bodies are already spending on consultations.

In studying the cases which have led to significant and important public policy and legislative changes (as well as those that have been less effective), there are a number of conditions that make success more likely:

- There needs to be a clear task connected to an existing policy agenda. However, engagement should happen early on, before an issue becomes a controversy.
- Political backing and engagement is crucial. Citizens want to have an impact. Having someone in a position to act on their recommendations and invite them to participate ensures that those willing to participate goes beyond the ranks of the already politically engaged, impassioned activist.
- There cannot be a predetermined outcome; numerous options should be within the realms of possibility. The logic of cynics is that this type of process is merely a way of legitimising a preferred decision. If people feel the issue was 'fixed' before the process began, it merely fuels greater distrust and disillusionment.
- Media engagement in the early phases is very important. The process cannot exist in isolation. If it is only internal, there is a risk of ignoring the results, which does not help solve the legitimacy problem.
- Time is imperative and one of the big differences with other public engagement processes. The average amount of time given to citizens across the 50 case studies was five full-day meetings over three months. The more time given for learning and deliberation, the better the results as citizens are able to provide more informed and considered views.
- Expertise provided by an independent organisation, dedicated to the methodological rigour of long-form deliberations, is crucial for the design, delivery and institutionalisation of these processes as a key tool available to public authorities for public decision-making.

Additionally, it is clear that long-form deliberative processes work particularly well for certain types of issues, in particular for resolving problems that involve difficult trade-offs and where priorities need to be identified. They are the opposite of a 'wish-list' consultation, where respondents are not required to consider others' ideas and proposals, or funding options for their ideas. This is one of the key strengths of mini-publics more generally: that participants develop an understanding of the constraints and dilemmas that are an inherent part of policymaking, rather than be infantilised in engagement processes where they do not get to learn about those constraints and thus are invited to produce unreflective wishful thinking. In the latter, decision-makers tend to dismiss unrealistic or unfeasible recommendations and paint 'the public' as misinformed or incompetent on public matters. This is merely a design flaw in public engagement processes, as exemplified by the cases of long-form deliberations, where time and resources are key correctives. People produce sensible, pragmatic ideas when treated as grown-ups.

Although not exhaustive, some of the main types of issues that long-form deliberative processes are particularly well-equipped to solve include:

- Infrastructure investment priorities;
- Planning and housing development options;
- Public health choices (i.e. obesity strategy, NHS reductions and restructuring, mental health strategies);
- Local fiscal decisions (i.e. decentralisation of business rates);
- Digital transition dilemmas (i.e. managing privacy concerns);
- Environmental questions;
- Constitutional matters.

Of course, it should be recognised that elected representatives still have a crucial role in any democracy. But this role has changed from its original purpose, established during a time when people travelled by horse and cart and wrote letters to communicate. An elected individual, to represent the views of others, made perfect sense in that context. Today, however, when many are active on social media, have their own blogs, travel with ease and can speak with others on the other side of the world, it is no wonder that elected representatives are no longer seen as the only people capable of solving problems.

Moreover, despite the critiques against royal commissions, inquiries and referendums, this is not an argument against ever using these methods for public decision-making. It is the notion that they are somehow superior to more deliberative forms of public engagement which is questioned here. Royal commissions and inquiries bring much-needed expertise on highly technical issues but can be complemented by long-form deliberations to inform citizens and to garner public support. It is also the case that referendums can be powerful means of authorising decisions. Yet, in order for referendums to deliver thoughtful outcomes, they should only be used at the end of an extended public deliberation, which may take place over months or years (a good example is the citizens' assembly model pioneered in Ontario and British Columbia on electoral reform), involving multiple long-form deliberations.

Canadian and Australian policymakers, politicians and civil servants have been leading the way in their recognition of the fact that the nature of politics is changing, utilising the wisdom of the public to make well-crafted policies that can command widespread popular support. When citizens collaborate, learn, empathise with experts and one another, sound public judgement is more likely to prevail. While efforts to use new forms of citizen engagement do exist in the UK, notably by innovative local councils and devolved parliaments, the benefits of the rigorous long-form deliberative approach are yet to be reaped, let alone institutionalised. The opportunity to do so is immense.

APPENDIX A

Canada case studies

Table A.   Canada case studies of long-form deliberative processes 2010–16

Level of government	Place	Year	Client	Panel name	Category	Topic	No. of participants	No. of invitations	Duration
City	Lethbridge	2016	Lethbridge City Council	Citizens' Assembly on Councillor Employment and Compensation	Political institutions	To consider whether Lethbridge city councillors should continue to serve on a part-time basis or whether they should fulfil their role on a full-time basis. The assembly will also provide guidance concerning their compensation	36	5,000	3 days
National	Canada	2016	Canadian Institues of Health Research	Citizens' Reference Panel on Pharmacare in Canada	Public health	To review provincial and federal policies concerning drug coverage and consider whether different models would better suit the needs of Canadians. The panel will issue a public report with its recommendations, to be shared with the federal health minister and her provincial and territorial counterparts	36	10,000	4 days
City	Toronto	2016–17	City of Toronto Planning Department	Toronto Planning Review Panel	Planning	To provide guidance concerning ongoing planning initiatives	28	12,000	12 days + 4 training days

City	Toronto	2016	St. Michael's Hospital	Residents' Health Services Panel	Public health	To help St. Michael's Hospital improve local health services available in their catchment area	28	14,500	8 days
City	Edmonton	2012–13	City of Edmonton's Office of Environment	Citizens' Panel on Edmonton's Energy and Climate Challenges	Climate	To make recommendations to administration and council, with the city's commitment that they will seriously consider their recommendations in developing an energy transition plan	56		6 days
City	Toronto	2016	St. Michael's Hospital	Academic Family Health Team Patient Design	Public health	To help the team improve the process and experience of a medical appointment	36	10,000	1 day
City	Calgary	2015	Calgary Chamber and City of Calgary	Calgary Commission on Municipal Infrastructure	Infrastructure investment	To review and propose revisions to the city's fiscal model	36	10,000	6 days
Regional	Halton	2015	Halton Region	Halton Region Citizens' Reference Panel on Strategic Priorities	Long-term plan	To review the region's work and additional directions for the 2015–2019 Strategic Action Plan	36	10,000	3 days
City	Toronto	2015	Metrolinx	Metrolinx Residents' Reference Panel on the Davenport Community Rail Overpass	Planning	To help inform the design process of a rail overpass in the Toronto community of Davenport	36	10,000	4 days + 1 evening

Table A. Canada case studies of long-form deliberative processes 2010–16 (cont. . .)

Level of government	Place	Year	Client	Panel name	Category	Topic	No. of participants	No. of invitations	Duration
City	Vancouver	2015	City of Vancouver	Grandview-Woodland Citizens' Assembly	Planning	To inform the development of a new 30-year Community Plan for Grandview-Woodland, a Vancouver neighbourhood	48	19,000	11 days
City	Toronto	2015	St. Joseph's Health Centre	St. Joseph's Health Centre Community Reference Panel	Public health	To create a series of recommendations and priorities to help inform the health centre's strategic plan	36	10,000	3 days + 1 evening
National	Canada	2015	Mental Health Commission of Canada	Citizens' Reference Panel on the Mental Health Action Plan for Canada	Public health	Recommending actions for inclusion in the MHAP	36	10,000	5 days
City	Toronto	2014	West Neighbourhood House and the Toronto Central Local Health Integration Network (LHIN)	Residents' Reference Panel on Supervised Injection Services	Public health	To propose recommendations to government on actions and guidelines for addressing public concern about the location and operation of potential injection services	36	16,500	4 days

Level	Location	Year	Organization	Panel	Topic	Purpose			Duration
Provincial	British Columbia	2013	Government of British Columbia	BC Services Card User Panel on Digital Services	Digital services plan	To create recommendations for the province's new digital services plan, which included a new, chip-enabled Services Card	36	16,500	4 days
Regional	Greater Toronto and Hamilton Area	2013	Metrolinx	Metrolinx Regional Residents' Reference Panel on Transport Investment	Infrastructure investment	To inform Metrolinx's strategy for raising funds to make long-term, sustainable investments in transit and transportation in the area	36	10,000	4 days
Regional	Prince Edward County	2013	Prince Edward County Council	Citizens' Assembly on the Size of the Council	Political institutions	To inform how many municipal councillors should represent the citizens of Prince Edward County	23	5,000	3 days
City	Edmonton	2012	City of Edmonton	Citizens' Panel on Food and Agriculture Planning in Edmonton	Agriculture	To discuss issues related to urban food and agriculture, deliberate over identified goals for this policy, and develop (and debate!) strategies for implementing activities to foster these goals	66		6 days
City	Calgary	2012	Calgary Arts Development Association	Calgary Arts Development Citizens' Reference Panel	Arts	To determine the future of art, art funding and the city's involvement in artistic communities	36	5,000	8 days

Table A. Canada case studies of long-form deliberative processes 2010–16 (cont. . .)

Level of government	Place	Year	Client	Panel name	Category	Topic	No. of participants	No. of invitations	Duration
Provincial	Ontario	2012	Ontario Ministry of Consumer Services	Ontario Ministry of Consumer Services Reference Panel on the Condominium Act	Housing	To create recommendations for updating the Condominium Act	36	10,000	3 days
City	Edmonton	2012	City of Edmonton	Citizens' Jury on Internet Voting	Political institutions	To deliver a verdict in favour or in opposition to the adoption of internet voting for Edmonton municipal elections	18		1 day
City	Hamilton	2011	City of Hamilton	Hamilton Citizens' Reference Panel on Cultural Policy and Planning	Culture	To inform Hamilton's new cultural plan	30	5,000	3 days
City	Toronto	2011	Toronto Community Housing Corporation	TCHC Tenant Communications Strategy and Tenants' Reference Panel	Housing	To ask residents how TCHC could improve the way it communicates with them	28	7,500	3 days
City	Toronto	2011	Diaspora Dialogues	Toronto Residents' Reference Panel on Household Income	Income inequality	To create recommendations for combating income inequality	44	7,500	3 days

City	Ottawa	2011	Ottawa Hospital	Ottawa Hospital Patients' Reference Panel on Clinical Services Transformation	Public health	To guide changes to Ottawa Hospital's cancer treatment programme	36	15,000	3 days
Provincial	Ontario	2011	PwC	Citizens' Reference Panel on Ontario Health Services	Public health	To learn about health care issues in Ontario and to develop a series of health care priorities	28	10,000	6 days
Regional	Halton	2011	Halton Region	Halton Region Citizens' Reference Panel on Strategic Priorities	Strategic city plan	To inform Halton's four-year strategic work plan	36	10,000	5 days
Regional	Champlain	2010	Champlain Local Health Integration Network	Champlain LHIN Citizens' Advisory Panel on Clinical Hospital Services Distribution Plan	Public health	To recommend possible models for distributing services among the Eastern Counties' hospitals	24	5,000	3 days
Provincial	Ontario	2010	Laidlaw Foundation	Ontario Youth Matter! Youth Advisory Council	Young people	To learn about current youth policies and propose recommendations for better involving young Ontarians in public policymaking		5,000	2 days

APPENDIX B

Australia case studies

Table B. Australia case studies of long-form deliberative processes 2012–16

Level of government	Place	Year	Client	Panel name	Category	Topic	No. of participants	No. of invitations	Duration
State	Victoria - Melbourne and Shepparton	2016	Government of Victoria	Infrastructure Victoria Citizens' Juries (x2)	Infrastructure investment	To develop recommendations for Infrastructure Victoria's 30-year plan for planning and investment decisions around which projects should be priorities for Victoria and how these projects should be paid for	43 (x2)	12,000	2-6 hours online, 5.5 days
State	South Australia	2016	South Australia's Department of the Premier and Cabinet	Nuclear Fuel Cycle Citizens' Jury	Nuclear waste	Should South Australia continue to pursue opportunities connected to the nuclear fuel cycle?	50 / 350	25,000	Jury one: 4 days; Jury two: 6 days
State	Victoria	2016	State Government of Victoria	Citizens' Jury on Democracy in Geelong	Political institutions	To recommend how the mayor, deputy mayor and councillors are elected; how many councillors should be elected and also specific comment about the municipality's representative structure	100	15,000	1 evening, 3 days

City	Greater Bendigo	2016	City of Greater Bendigo	City of Greater Bendigo Citizens' Jury	Strategic city plan	To identify the areas of common ground in the local community to inform the city's new council plan for key strategic issues	24	3,000	2 days, 4 evenings
City	Eurobodalla	2016	Eurobodalla Shire Council	Eurobodalla Citizens' Jury	Strategic city plan	To identify the areas of common ground in the local community to inform the city's new council plan for key strategic issues	24	3,000	2 days, 4 evenings
City	Noosa	2015	Noosa Shire Council	Noosa Community Jury	Environment/ Reducing organic waste	To consider trade-offs involved of environment benefit vs cost to citizens of reducing organic waste sent to landfill	24	3,000	6 evenings
State	Victoria	2015	VicHealth	Victoria's Citizens' Jury on Obesity	Public health	How can we make it easier to eat better?	100	20,000	7-8 hours online, 2 days
City	Penrith	2015	Penrith City Council	Penrith City Community Panel	Strategic city plan	To provide the council with a set of recommendations on what services and infrastructure are needed in Penrith and to what level of quality, and how they should be paid for	34	5,000	3-4 hours online, 5.5 days

Table B. Australia case studies of long-form deliberative processes 2012–16 (cont. . .)

Level of government	Place	Year	Client	Panel name	Category	Topic	No. of participants	No. of invitations	Duration
City	Canada Bay	2014	City of Canada Bay	City of Canada Bay Policy Panel	Council facilities	To provide policy advice to council on lease conditions fair for the proposed use where council-owned buildings are formally leased to third parties for their sole use on a discounted or subsidised community basis	24	4,000	6 days
State	South Australia	2014	South Australia's Department of the Premier and Cabinet	Sharing the Roads Safely Citizens' Jury	Cycling infrastructure	Motorists and cyclists will always be using our roads. What things could we trial to ensure they share the roads safely?	37	6,000	5 days
City	Marrickville	2014	Marrickville Council	Marrickville Infrastructure Jury	Infrastructure investment	To agree local priorities for public infrastructure	30	3,000	4 days, 1 evening
City	Moorebank	2014	Moorebank Intermodal Company	Moorebank Intermodal Citizens' Jury	Infrastructure investment	To determine how $1m should be spent to benefit the local community	30	4,000	5 days
City	Darebin	2014	Darebin City Council	Darebin Participatory Budgeting Citizens' Jury	Infrastructure investment	To propose infrastructure developments for supporting disadvantaged areas of the community	43	3,000	4 days

State	South Australia	2014	South Australia's Department of Environment, Water and Natural Resources	Community Panel for South East Drainage	Infrastructure investment	To provide the minister for sustainability, environment and conservation with an actionable recommendation as to how to pay for maintenance of the drainage system	24	7,000	6 days
City	Noosa	2014	Noosa Shire Council	Noosa Community Jury	River management	River management	24	3,000	6 days
City	Melbourne	2014	City of Melbourne	Melbourne People's Panel	Strategic city plan	To develop recommendations for the city's 10-year financial plan	43	7,000	6 days
City	Sydney	2013	Thomas Kelly Youth Foundation	Safe and Vibrant Nightlife Citizens' Jury	Safe and vibrant nightlife	To explore whether common ground can be found as to reform options which balance community safety and personal freedom to achieve a safe and vibrant nightlife in Sydney	43	20,000	6 days

Table B. Australia case studies of long-form deliberative processes 2012–16 (cont...)

Level of government	Place	Year	Client	Panel name	Category	Topic	No. of participants	No. of invitations	Duration
City	Adelaide	2013	Department of Premier and Cabinet	Safe and Vibrant Nightlife Citizens' Jury	Safe and vibrant nightlife	To explore whether common ground can be found as to reform options which balance community safety and personal freedom to achieve a safe and vibrant nightlife in Adelaide	43	24,000	5 days
State	New South Wales - Sydney and Tamworth	2012	New South Wales Government	Citizens' Jury on Energy Generation (x2)	Energy	To find common ground in the community about the potential for, and barriers to, development of alternative forms of energy generation (i.e. tidal, geothermal) in NSW	45 (x2)	4,000	4 days
City	Canada Bay	2012	City of Canada Bay	City of Canada Bay Citizens' Panel	Service delivery	What services should the city deliver and how should we pay for them?	36	1,500	5 days

REFERENCES

Acemoglu, Daron and James A. Robinson. 2012. *Why Nations Fail: The Origins of Power, Prosperity and Poverty*. London: Profile Books Ltd.

Ansell, Chris and Alison Gash. 2008. 'Collaborative governance in theory and practice'. *Journal of Public Administration Research and Theory* 18 (8): 543–71.

Better Together. 2015. *Better Together: Bringing Citizens into Government Decision-making*. Government of South Australia. Available at: http://yoursay.sa.gov.au/media/W1siZiIsIjIwMTUvMDMvMTMvMDBfMjVfNDJfNDc3X0JldHRlcl9Ub2dldGhlcl9Ccm9jaHVyZV9kaWdpdGFsLnBkZiJdXQ/Better%20Together%20Brochure%20digital.pdf.

British Columbia Ministry of Technology, Innovation and Citizens' Services. 2014. *Digital Services Consultation – Fall 2013 Minister's Response*. Available at: http://www.gov.bc.ca/citz/down/DigitalServicesConsultation_report_web.pdf.

British Columbia Services Card User Panel. 2013. *Recommendations from the B.C. Services Card User Panel*. Toronto: MASS LBP. Available at: http://engage.gov.bc.ca/digitalservices/files/2014/03/Appendix-II-Recomendations-from-BC-Services-Card-User-Panel-Final.pdf.

Chandler, Mark. 2017. 'Heathrow Expansion: Government spent "eye-watering" £10k a day on consultants over third runway'. *The Evening Standard*. 2 January 2017.

Chwalisz, Claudia. 2015. *The Populist Signal: Why Politics and Democracy Need to Change*. London: Rowman & Littlefield International.

Citizens' Reference Panel on Pharmacare in Canada. 2016. About the Panel. Available at: http://www.crppc-gccamp.ca/.

City of Melbourne. 2015. *10 Year Financial Plan 2015–2025*. Available at: http://participate.melbourne.vic.gov.au/application/files/1314/3640/5781/City_of_Melbourne_10_Year_Financial_Plan.pdf.

City of Toronto. 2016. Introducing the Inaugural Toronto Planning Review Panel. Toronto: City of Toronto.

Dalton, Russell J. and Steven Weldom. 2013. 'Is direct democracy a kinder and gentler democracy?'. *Taiwan Journal of Democracy*, Special Issue: 39–62.

Dalton, Russell J. 2008. *Citizen Politics: Public Opinion and Political Parties in Advanced Industrial Democracies*. Thousand Oaks, CA: Sage Publications.

Delap, Clare. 2001. 'Citizens' juries: Reflections on the UK experience'. *PLA Notes 40*. Available at: pubs.iied.org/pdfs/G01929.pdf.

Donaldson, David. 2016. 'VicHealth's citizens' jury lessons: no censorship, impartiality'. *The Mandarin*. Available at: http://www.themandarin.com.au/65180-vic-healths-citizens-jury-lessons-no-censorship-impartiality/?utm_source=The%20Juice%20-%20combined%20list&pgnc=1.

Douglas, Mary. 1986. *How Institutions Think*. Syracuse, NY: Syracuse U. Press.

Elstub, Stephen and Oliver Escobar. Eds. Forthcoming 2018. *The Handbook of Democratic Innovation and Governance*. Cheltenham, UK; Northampton, MA, USA: Edward Elgar.

EU Referendum Polling. Electoral Reform Society. Available at: http://www.electoral-reform.org.uk/eu-referendum-polling. Accessed on 5 May 2016.

Farazmand, Ali. 2012. 'Sound governance: Engaging citizens through collaborative organizations'. *Public Organization Review* 12: 223–41.

Farrell, David M. 2014. '"Stripped down" or reconfigured democracy'. *West European Politics* 37 (2): 439–55.

Fischer Frank. 2016. 'Participatory governance: From theory to practice'. In Fainstein, Susan and James DeFilippis, Eds. *Readings in Planning Theory*, Oxford: John Wiley & Sons, Ltd.

Fishkin, James S. 2008. 'Consulting the public—thoughtfully'. In *Governance Reform under Real-World Conditions: Citizens, Stakeholders, and Voice*, Eds. Sina Odugbemi and Thomas Jacobson. Washington, DC: World Bank.

Fishkin, James S. 2009. *When the People Speak: Deliberative Democracy and Public Consultation*. Oxford: Oxford University Press.

Flinders, Matthew, Katie Ghose, Will Jennings, Edward Molloy, Brenton Prosser, Alan Renwick, Graham Smith and Paolo Spada. 2016. *Democracy Matters: Lessons from the 2015 Citizens' Assemblies on English Devolution*.

Fung, Archon. 2015. 'Putting the public back into governance: The challenges of citizen participation and its future'. *Public Administration Review* 75 (4): 513–22.

Fung, Archon. 2006. Varieties of Participation in Complex Governance. Special issue, *Public Administration Review* 66: 66–75.

Fung, Archon and Erik Olin Wright. 2003. 'Deepening democracy: Innovations in empowered participatory governance'. *Politics & Society* 29: 5–41.

Goodin, Robert E. and John Dryzek. 2006. 'Deliberative impacts: The macro-political uptake of mini-publics'. *Politics & Society* 34 (2): 219–44.

Grant, John. 2013. 'Canada's republican invention? On the political theory and practice of citizens' assemblies'. *Political Studies* 62 (3): 539–55.

Gray, Barbara. 2000. 'Assessing inter-organizational collaboration: multiple conceptions and multiple methods'. In D. Faulkner & M. de Rond, Eds. *Perspectives on Collaboration*. Oxford: Oxford University Press.

Grönlund, Kimmo, André Bächtiger and Maija Setälä. Eds. 2014. *Deliberative Mini-Publics: Involving Citizens in the Democratic Process*. Colchester: ECPR Press.

Gurin, J. 2014. 'Open governments, open data: A new lever for transparency, citizen engagement, and economic growth'. *SAIS Review of International Affairs* 34 (1): 71–82.

Hendriks, Carolyn M. 2016. 'Coupling citizens and elites in deliberative systems: The role of institutional design. *European Journal of Political Research* 55: 43–60.

Ilott, Oliver and Emma Norris. 2015. *Smarter Engagement: Harnessing Public Voice in Policy Challenges*. London: Institute for Government. Available at: http://www.instituteforgovernment.org.uk/sites/default/files/publications/4483%20IFG%20-%20Smarter%20Engagement%20v5.pdf.

Infrastructure Victoria. 2016. *Your Considered Opinion: Response to Consultation on Options and Recommendations from the Citizen Juries*. Victoria: State of Victoria. Available at: http://yoursay.infrastructurevictoria.com.au/30-year-strategy/application/files/4014/7545/9749/Your_Considered_Opinion_-_Final_Web.PDF.

Involve. 2005. *The True Costs of Public Participation*. London: Involve.

Johns, Melissa Marie and Valentina Saltane. 2016. 'Citizen engagement in rulemaking – Evidence on regulatory practices in 185 countries'. Policy Research working paper; no. WPS 7840. Washington, D.C.: World Bank Group.

Kao, A.B. and I.D. Couzin. 2014. 'Decision accuracy in complex environments is often maximized by small group sizes'. *Proceedings of the Royal Society* 281: 1784.

Knack, Stephen, and Paul J. Zak. 2003. 'Building trust: Public policy, interpersonal trust, and economic development'. *Supreme Court Economic Review* 10: 91–107.

Johnston, Stephanie. 2013. 'The worst form of government'. *The Adelaide Review*. Available at: http://adelaidereview.com.au/opinion/politics-opinion/the-worst-form-of-government/.

Lafont, Cristina. 2014. 'Deliberation, participation and democratic legitimacy: Should deliberative mini-publics shape public policy?' *Journal of Political Philosophy* 18 (1): 64–100.

Landemore, Helene E. 2012. 'Why the many are smarter than the few and why it matters'. *Journal of Public Deliberation* 8 (1): Article 7.

Leach, William D. and Paul A. Sabatier. 2005. 'To trust an adversary: Integrating rational and psychological models of collaborative policy-making'. *American Political Science Review* 99: 491–503.

Leadbeater, Charlie. 2014. *The Frugal Innovator: Creating Change on a Shoestring Budget*. London: Palgrave Macmillan UK.

LeDuc, Lawrence. 2011. 'Electoral reform and direct democracy in Canada: When citizens become involved'. *West European Politics* 34 (3): 551–57.

Legislative Assembly of New South Wales. 2012. *The Economics of Energy Generation*. Sydney, New South Wales. Available at: http://www.newdemocracy.com.au/docs/activeprojects/PAC_EconomicsofEnergyGenerationRep6_55November2012.pdf.

Lenihan, Don. 2014. *A Case Study of Canada's Condominium Act Review*. Ottawa: Public Policy Forum.

Maer, Lucinda. 2007. 'Citizens' juries'. Standard Note: SN/PC/04546. London: House of Commons Library.

Mair, Peter. 2013. *Ruling the Void: The Hollowing of Western Democracy*. London: Verso.

Mair, Peter. 2009. 'Representative versus responsible government'. Max-Planck-Institute Working Paper. Cologne: Max-Planck-Institute. Available at: http://www.mpifg.de/pu/workpap/wp09-8.pdf.

Manin, Bernard. 1987. 'On legitimacy and political deliberation'. Translated by Elly Stein and Jane Mansbridge. *Political Theory* 15 (3): 338–68.

Mansbridge, Jane. 2012. 'On the importance of getting things done'. *Political Science and Politics* 45 (1): 1–8.

MASS LBP. 2013. *The Ontario Residents' Panel to Review the Condominium Act.* Prepared by MASS LBP for Public Policy Forum.

MASS LBP. 2013. *Residents' Reference Panel on Regional Transportation Investment.* Prepared by MASS LBP for Metrolinx. Available at: http://www.metrolinx.com/en/regionalplanning/funding/IS_Appendix_E_EN.pdf.

Melbourne People's Panel. 2014. *10 Year Financial Plan People's Panel Report.* Available at: http://www.newdemocracy.com.au/docs/activeprojects/City%20of%20Melbourne%20Peoples%20Panel%20Recommendations%20November%202014.pdf.

Mental Health Commission of Canada. 2016. *Recommendations from the Citizens Reference Panel on the Mental Health Action Plan for Canada.* Ottawa: Mental Health Commission of Canada. Available at: http://www.mentalhealthcommission.ca/English/media/3745.

Metropolitan Citizen Jury. 2016. Infrastructure Victoria Metropolitan Citizen Jury Report. Available at: http://yoursay.infrastructurevictoria.com.au/30-year-strategy/application/files/7914/7018/2665/Metropolitan_Citizen_Jury_report.pdf.

Molony, Lee-Anne. 2015. *Evaluation of the Community Engagement Process for the 10 Year Financial Plan.* Melbourne: Clear Horizon Consulting. Available at: http://participate.melbourne.vic.gov.au/application/files/3514/4477/8217/Evaluation_of_community_engagement_for_the_10_Year_Financial_Plan.pdf.

Naím, Moisés. 2013. *The End of Power: From Boardrooms to Battlefields and Churches to States, Why Being in Charge isn't What it Used to be.* New York, NY.: Basic Books.

New South Wales Government. 2013. *Legislative Assembly Public Accounts Committee Inquiry into the Economics of Energy Generation Public Report 6/55: NSW Government Response.* Available at: http://www.newdemocracy.com.au/docs/activeprojects/PAC_economics_of_energy_generation_6-55.pdf.

Nuclear Fuel Cycle Citizens' Jury. 2016. Final Report – Raw Final Text. Available at: http://www.newdemocracy.com.au/docs/activeprojects/sanuclearjury/Nuclear%20Fuel%20Cycle%20Citizens%20Jury%20-%20Final%20Report%20%E2%80%93%20Raw%20Final%20Text%20-%20Sunday%20July%2010th%20340pm.pdf.

OECD (Organisation for Economic Co-operation and Development). 2009. *Focus on Citizens: Public Engagement for Better Policy and Services.* OECD Studies on Public Engagement. Paris: OECD Publishing.

Owen, David and Graham Smith. 2015. 'Survey article: Deliberation, democracy and the systemic turn'. *Journal of Political Philosophy* 23 (2): 213–34.

Page, Scott E. 2008. *The Difference: How the Power of Diversity Creates Better Groups, Firms, Schools, and Societies.* New Jersey: Princeton University Press.

Patemen, Carole. 2012. 'Participatory democracy revisited'. *Perspectives on Politics* 10 (1): 7–19.

Przeworski, Adam, Susan Stokes and Bernard Manin, Eds. 1999. *Democracy, Accountability, and Representation.* New York: Cambridge University Press.

Public Inquiries, Inquests, Royal Commissions, Reviews and Investigations. The National Archives. Available at: http://www.nationalarchives. gov.uk/webarchive/inquiries-inquests-royal-commissions.htm#a.

Regional Citizen Jury. 2016. *Infrastructure Victoria Regional Citizen Jury Report.* Available at: http://yoursay.infrastructurevictoria.com.au/30-year-strategy/application/files/8014/7020/7151/Regional_citizen_jury_report_final.pdf.

Riddell, Peter. 2013. *Be Careful What You Review.* London: Institute for Government. Available at: http://www.instituteforgovernment.org.uk/blog/6086/be-careful-what-you-review/.

Riddell, Peter and Pepita Barlow. 2013. *The Lost World of Royal Commissions.* London: Institute for Government. Available at: http://www.institute forgovernment.org.uk/blog/6069/the-lost-world-of-royal-commissions/.

Roberts, Jennifer and Oliver Escobar. 2015. *Involving Communities in Deliberation: A Study of 3 Citizens' Juries on Onshore Wind Farms in Scotland.* Available at: http://www.climatexchange.org.uk/files/5614/3213/1663/Citizens_Juries_-_Full_Report.pdf.

Rogers, Ellen and Edward P. Weber. 2010. 'Thinking harder about outcomes for collaborative governance arrangements'. *American Review of Public Administration* 40 (5): 546–67.

Rosanvallon, Pierre. 2015. *Le Bon Gouvernement.* Paris: Seuil.

Rosanvallon, Pierre. 2008. *La contre-démocratie. La politique à l'âge de la défiance.* Paris: Seuil.

Rosanvallon, Pierre. 2008. *La Légitimité démocratique. Impartialité, réflexivité, proximité.* Paris: Seuil.

Sharma, Bhavna. 2008. *Voice, Accountability and Civic Engagement: A Conceptual Overview*. Paper commissioned by Oslo Governance Centre, Bureau for Development Policy, United Nations Development Programme. London: Overseas Development Institute.

Smith, Graham and David Owen. 2015. 'Deliberation, Democracy, and the Systemic Turn'. *The Journal of Political Philosophy* 23 (2): 213–34.

Smith, Graham and Matthew Ryan. 2014. 'Defining mini-publics: Making sense of existing conceptions'. In *Deliberative Mini-Publics: Involving Citizens in the Democratic Process*, Eds. Kimmo Grönlund, André Bächtiger and Maija Setälä. Colchester, UK: ECPR Press.

Smith, Graham. 2009. *Democratic Innovations: Designing Institutions for Citizen Participation*. Cambridge: Cambridge University Press.

Social Mobility and Poverty Commission. 2014. *Elitist Britain?* London: Gov.uk. Available at: https://www.gov.uk/government/uploads/system/uploads/attachment_data/file/347915/Elitist_Britain_-_Final.pdf.

South Australia Government. 2015. *Citizens' Jury: Vibrant and Safe Adelaide Nightlife – January 2015 Status Update on New Initiatives Arising from Citizens' Jury Recommendations*. Available at: http://assets.yoursay.sa.gov.au/production/2015/01/09/00_14_50_113_Status_update_January_2015_on_new_initiatives.pdf.

South Australia Government. 2013. *The State Government Response to the Recommendations of South Australia's First Citizens' Jury*. Available at: http://www.newdemocracy.com.au/docs/activeprojects/SACitizensJury_StateGovernmentResponse.pdf.

Stoker, Gerry and Mark Evans. 2014. 'The "democracy-politics paradox": The dynamics of political alienation'. *Democratic Theory* 1 (2): 26–36.

Stoker, Gerry. 2004. *Designing Institutions for Governance in Complex Environments: Normative Rational Choice and Cultural Institutional Theories Explored and Contrasted*. Economic and Social Research Council Fellowship Paper No. 1.

Suiter, Jane, David M. Farrell, and Eoin O'Malley. 2014. 'When do deliberative citizens change their opinions? Evidence from the Irish Citizens' Assembly'. *International Political Science Review*: 1–15.

Suiter, Jane, David M. Farrell, and Eoin O'Malley. 2012. *Is Deliberation for Everyone? Variations in the Capacities of Participants in an Irish Deliberative Experiment*. APSA 2012 Annual Meeting Paper.

Taylor, Matthew. 2016. 'Towards a Fully Engaged Organisation'. RSA blog. Available at: https://www.thersa.org/discover/publications-and-articles/matthew-taylor-blog/2016/01/towards-a-fully-engaged-organisation.

Torriti, Jacopo. 2007. '(Regulatory) Impact Assessments in the European Union: A tool for better regulation, less regulation or less bad regulation?'. *Journal of Risk Research* 10 (2): 239–76.

VicHealth. 2016. *Victoria's Citizens' Jury on Obesity Insights Report 2016.* Melbourne: Victorian Health Promotion Foundation.

White, Hannah. 2015. *Select Committees Under Scrutiny: Case Studies from the 2010–15 Parliament.* London: Institute for Government. Available at: http://www.instituteforgovernment.org.uk/sites/default/files/publications/Under%20scrutiny%20case%20studies%20final_0.pdf.

Zakaras, Alex. 2010. 'Lot and democratic representation: A modest proposal'. *Constellations* 17 (3).